Moxietown

Jim Baumer

Copyright © 2008 by Jim Baumer

Inquiries regarding requests to reprint all or part of Moxietown should be directed to RiverVision Press at:

RiverVision Press
P.O. Box 1136
Lewiston, Maine 04243-1136

RiverVision Press is a Maine-based small press, specializing in books about Maine and its unique culture and heritage. Our focus is on history, memoir and other styles that capture the spirit of Maine. RiverVision Press strives to be a press that captures a side of Maine that has been lost, forgotten, or never known.

Cover design by Ari Meil. Cover photo © RiverVision Press

Moxie Cover Collage is used by permission of James Jansson

RiverVision Press   www.rivervisionpress.com

Moxie is a registered trademark of Cornucopia Beverages Company, Bedford, New Hampshire

This book is dedicated to
Moxie drinkers everywhere

circa 1930
Moxie Horsemobile

Acknowledgements

Whenever you write a book, there are a wealth of people who assist and guide you along the way, particularly when you write nonfiction.

While this book isn't as research-driven as the first one, it still required source materials, stories, and input from countless people. I always come away grateful, as well as humbled, by the graciousness that people exhibit, when you tell them you are working on a book.

First and foremost, I want to thank my wife, Mary. Anyone that lives with a writer knows that we are odd creatures, given to strange hours of sleep, or no sleep at all. During those four to six weeks prior to deadline, it is best to leave us alone, and not ask much about details, unless we care to share them. Thanks, Mary, for understanding, and allowing me the space and time to pursue my passion of writing.

This book was truly a family affair, as my son, Mark, and his girlfriend, Gabi Goodman, had a big hand in the process. After many years of sharing a bond through baseball, Mark and I now have mutual interests in writing and publishing. Mark's become a valuable editorial foil, copy editor, and offered needed support during those times of self-doubt. Gabi (and Mark) spent a Saturday, doing a photo shoot at Kennebec's and shooting countless photos of the town. A talented photographer, several of Gabi's photos will be used in this book, as well as the full-length, which will be out in the fall.

Speaking of families, my parents have become my biggest fans. My mom, Helen, is a force to be reckoned with on the sales and marketing side of things. My father, Herman, offered stories, memories, and verification of various details about the town of Lisbon.

I want to thank the wonderful people of Lisbon Falls, my hometown. Frank Anicetti was always ready to help with a story, or add details about Moxie and how it connects to the town. The day I interviewed him, President's Day, in February, he was dealing with a leaking roof, but never missed a beat in our interview, other than to empty a pail. I also got to see him in action when a young couple, from Kennebunk, dropped by, as if on cue, to inquire about Moxie, because they'd heard about some store in Lisbon Falls that was Moxie headquarters.

If Frank is the Moxie Man, then Sue Conroy is the Queen of Moxie. Since 2000, Sue's been putting together the details, and all the logistics of the town's annual festival. I never knew how much went into the festival, until 2004, when I joined the Moxie Committee, to help with PR and marketing. Sue's love for the town and its people is manifested the second weekend every July. We got to share a Sunday afternoon, in March, talking about what goes into making the festival happen, and why she puts so much passion into making it all happen each year. I'd also be remiss if I didn't mention Sue's son, Toby. He's become an essential part of putting on the festival each and every year. Unfortunately, I didn't get a chance to get his perspective on the festival, but we've made plans to catch up and I'm sure you'll hear more from Toby when the full-length book is released, in October.

Dealing with stories and the history of any subject requires research, which is time-consuming, and often difficult. The Lisbon Historical Society, and in particular, Dot Smith, have been unbelievably helpful in providing a wealth of material about the town, as well as pointing me towards others, who might have additional information. On several occasions, Dot's opened the archives for me on Saturday, to accommodate my schedule. Many of the book's photos came from their vast collection of town photos, particularly of Moxie Festivals from the past. Dot's husband, Al, was always patient with me when he came by to pick up Dot, and we were in the midst of making copies of articles, or scanning "just a few more photos." Bill Barr, Society Treasurer, as well as assistant archivist, was always quick to chime in with a story about the town's past.

This book, about Moxie, took me outside the confines of Lisbon proper. One group of Moxie aficionados that were exceptionally helpful was the New England Moxie Congress (NEMC). President Merrill Lewis granted me an interview, at his home. Merrill's passion for Moxie, as well as his championing of the Congress's work was obvious. Congress historian, John Lehaney, spoke with me from Missouri, providing me with a sense of who the NEMC is, and why people are part of it, as well as emailing and mailing material to me. NEMC member, Jim Jansson, who many have seen doing his live Moxie Boy routine, during the festival, was especially gracious in sending along material that saved me hours of research. He mailed his yet unpublished book, *The Stories Behind The Moxie Collage,* which details how he put together four wonderful collages from prior Moxie Festivals.

Jansson's 4th annual edition, "Merrill's sneakers—The Spirit of St. Lewis," is what was utilized for the book's front cover. When Jansson mailed this to me, I immediately knew this could be the cover. Jansson was gracious enough to allow me to use it.

Justin Conroy, brand manager for Cornucopia, granted me the chance to ask about their acquisition of the Moxie brand, as well as what the company's plans are for Moxie, in the future. Conroy was very generous with his time and I've included our entire interview, almost verbatim, because it was so good.

Fred Goldrup, who many festival-goers know as Taurus the Clown, shared wonderful stories about how Taurus came to be, as well as how he came to be the catalyst behind having Moxie recognized at the state's official soft drink.

Gary Crocker, Maine humorist, and lifetime member of the NEMC, sent me a great photo of the Moxie bus, somewhere in Jackman, Maine. Gary also provided a great Moxie story, as well as offering encouragement to me as a writer.

Q. David Bowers, the author of *The Moxie Encyclopedia, Volume I, The History*, kindly gave me permission to utilize any of his extensive source material in this amazing compendium of Moxie history and lore. As a researcher, I can only imagine the time and effort that Bowers put into this project. To be so accommodating to a fellow author speaks volumes about him as a person, and I'm indebted to him for leaving clear markers for others, along the Moxie highway.

Independent publishing can be a solitary existence. About two years ago, I met fellow publisher, Ari Meil, of Warren Machine Company. Ari's became a colleague and friend, sharing tips, encouragement and with this project, adding his design experience to the process. Thanks, Ari.

Sometimes it takes a village to write a book and the village of Lisbon—made up of the three communities of Lisbon Falls, Lisbon Center, and Lisbon—provided me with a wealth of material, not only for *Moxietown*, but for the full length, *Moxie Matters: Life's Beginnings in a Small Maine Town*, which will be out in the fall. I love the town and for what it's instilled in me; a love of community, a firsthand knowledge of the people that make up small Maine towns, as well as a sense of what values are most important in life.

Jim Baumer
May, 2008

CONTENTS

Introduction

Back in 2004, I set out to write my first book, *When Towns Had Teams*. Having never written a book before, the process was new and I was in foreign territory.

Fast forward to 2007; my first book had won an IPPY, awarded by Independent Publisher, for Best Nonfiction Title in the Northeast, in 2006. I had moved on to publishing another writer's work, which was fraught with its own issues and perils. It also kept me away from doing what I started RiverVision Press for in the first place—to bring my own books to market.

During the fall, I began considering ideas for my next book. I wanted to capture aspects of what it was like growing up in small town Maine, in the late 1960s and early 1970s, one of the last great times in Maine to be a kid.

The town that I grew up in, Lisbon Falls, has always held a special place in my heart. When I moved away during the early 80s, I missed that special place that had been my hometown. Like many, I had to leave it, to really appreciate the special character that it held. Remembering that place became my focus as I started those first few tentative steps towards creating a manuscript that eventually would be another book.

While there are many different elements that capture what Lisbon Falls means to me, the annual Moxie Festival, which happens every July, was something that I knew I wanted to delve into, as part of my research for the new book.

My intent was to create a chapter or two about Moxie, and then move on to other aspects of the town. Starting with the creation of my own concise, but complete history of the drink, I next wanted to help readers understand how the town of Lisbon became the epicenter of the Moxie universe. To do that, I knew an interview with Frank Anicetti, the Moxie Man, was in order.

Shortly after Christmas, I began considering the possibility of shortening my timeline for the project and shoot for next year's Moxie Festival to release my new book. Setting tight deadlines for yourself is certainly one way to ensure that you get your books to market. It's also a great way to lose your mind, and jeopardize your marriage.

When it became obvious in early 2008 that I was not going to have my full-length book, *Moxie Matters: Life's Beginnings in a Small Maine Town*, ready for Moxie, I had to come up with an alternative plan. Interestingly, my two chapters about Moxie had taken on a new energy and I had developed some additional ideas for new angles about Moxie that no one had looked at before. Also, as I delved into the two books written by Frank Potter, and Q. David Bowers' extensive and thorough, *The Moxie Encyclopedia, Volume I*, I recognized that there was still a wealth of Moxie ground not traveled before.

After my interview with Anicetti in February, I scheduled time to talk with Sue Conroy, who has spearheaded the festival in town, since 2000. That interview helped create some new avenues to explore and by early March, I had four complete chapters and designs on one or two more. I also had made the decision to release my Moxie material in a special, limited pressing edition, to commemorate the town's 25th anniversary of the Moxie Festival.

Moxietown is my contribution to the history and lore of Moxie. For a drink that's been around for over one-hundred years, surprisingly, there have only been three significant books written on the subject. As I found out in my research, there is plenty of material that can still be covered, and with fans like many of the members of the New England Moxie Congress, and others, there is a demand for books that are well-written and handle the subject with care.

I hope readers enjoy my own personal take on Moxie. I'm pleased to be the first writer to detail how Lisbon Falls assumed its place as a Moxie destination, each July (and during other times of the year). To my knowledge, I'm the only one that has documented the Potter book signing, as well as clarifying the dates, as to why this summer's festival is the 25th. Kudos to Frank Anicetti for helping me with the math on that one.

It's been over 20 years since a significant work has been added to Moxie's limited canon. *Moxietown* is a unique twist on the drink's one-hundred plus year saga.

While Moxie is a soft drink, it's also a state of mind and in my opinion, represents an element of Americana that is becoming harder to locate in our rapidly changing culture.

Drink Moxie!

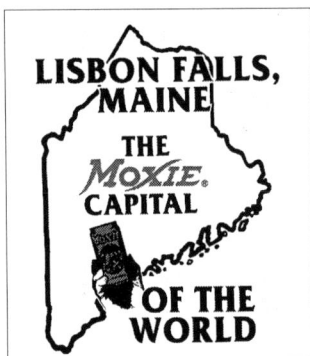

LISBON FALLS,
MAINE

THE
MOXIE®
CAPITAL

OF THE
WORLD

Welcome to Moxietown

Chapter 1
A Somewhat Brief History of Moxie

Its beginnings

In the latter days of the 19th century, the development of patent medicines was a popular pursuit of fledgling inventors, backroom chemists, and other assorted types. Long before the days of branding and Madison Avenue marketing, these various products often burst on the scene to much fanfare and quickly faded from view, only to become future trivia questions and left solely to the most loyal of consumers who in their own right could be described as cult aficionados.

Located in the Merrimack Valley of Massachusetts, the city of Lowell in the 1880s was an industrial city, with huge textile facilities lining the Merrimack River. While textile production was the anchor industry of the area, numerous manufacturers of patent medicines and various elixirs also set up shop in the city.

On July 16, 1885, Dr. Augustin Thompson filed trademark number 12,565 (subsequently registered on September 8, 1885) for a product he called Moxie Nerve Food.

Thompson's trademark indicated that Moxie, "has not a drop of Medicine, Poison, Stimulant, or Alcohol in its composition."

Later on, Thompson's application stated that Moxie was, "a liquid preparation charged with soda for the cure of paralysis, softening of the brain, and mental imbecility and called

'Moxie Nerve Food.' It is comprised in the class of medical compounds."

The trademark application specified that Thompson chose the word Moxie arbitrarily and that he had been using the term in his business to describe his drink since April 1, 1884. Later, Moxie collectors and other historians would split hairs about whether the drink originated in 1884 or 1885. For marketing purposes, at least from the 1940s onward, ads stated that Moxie had been around since 1884.

After the filing of his patent for his product, Thompson began thinking of ways to market his drink/elixir, which led to the legend of something know as Lieutenant Moxie.

Lieutenant Moxie was a friend of Dr. Thompson. He had amassed a considerable fortune through speculation in oil around the world. After acquiring tubercular consumption from his mother, Moxie traveled to various regions of the world in search of a cure. In the mountains of South America, he discovered a medicinal plant, later known to be gentian root, being used by natives, to cure various ailments. Finding that it elicited a positive reaction on his own nervous system, Thompson claims the Lieutenant shipped a supply of the medicinal root, with the history of its use, to him in Lowell.

Thompson noted, "I found it cured anything caused by nervous exhaustion. It restored nervous people who were tired out mentally or physically; stopped the appetite for intoxicants in old drunkards, insanity, blindness from overtaxing the sight, paralysis, all but hereditary sick-headache, loss of manhood from excesses, made people able to stand twice their usual amount of labor, mentally, or physically, with less fatique. It cured two cases of softening of the brain, and recovered helpless limbs. I found it to be neither medicine nor stimulant, but a nerve food, and harmless as milk." [from *The Moxie Encyclopedia, Volume I, The History,* by Q. David Bowers, page 32.]

News spread quickly of claims of Moxie's medicinal qualities and demand for Thompson's product saw him begin production, bottling 27,000 bottles per week.

What began as a local phenomenon, quickly expanded beyond the soda fountains and stores of Lowell. By July of 1885, Moxie was made in four large factories, with distribution throughout New England and New York. Production now exceeded 500,000 bottles. Wholesale dealers were being added all the time and sales agents were acquired in Rochester, New York; Baltimore, Maryland; and as far west as Chicago, Illinois.

While numerous variations on the Moxie legend would appear over the next several decades, it was obvious that Thompson's original product had struck a nerve with consumers in New England and elsewhere. Where Thompson garnered the Moxie name from will always be a point of conjecture, particularly whether, or not, Moxie was a name that originated from Maine geography.

One thing we do know is that Dr. Augustin Thompson was born in Union, Maine, on November 25, 1835. It's possible that he remembered seeing the name Moxie on a map of the state, like Moxie Lake, Moxie Mountain, or East Moxie Township.

Thompson received his education in the public schools of Union and at the age of sixteen, became an apprentice for a blacksmith. Young Thompson tried to develop a passion for his new trade, but he found it too confining and never was able to put his whole being into it.

As was common of self-taught men from the era, young Thompson spent much time studying a variety of books. He taught himself Latin and German and his once small library continued to expand. A voracious reader, Thompson acquired books wherever he could find them.

As an adult, Thompson would stand five feet, ten inches tall and by the time of the Civil War, though he might have been perceived as something of an intellectual, he was still able to mix it up with the best of his Company G of the 28th infantry. Known as the Maine Volunteers, Thompson did his part after enlisting in September of 1862, and was even commended twice for gallant performances in battle.

During one such battle, Thompson was struck in the chest by a rifle butt and subsequently was diagnosed with tuberculosis. From the complications that came with the disease, Thompson received an honorable discharge and returned to Maine in August of 1863.

After the war, Thompson enrolled at Hahnemann Homeopathic College in Philadelphia, where he would study medicine and graduate at the head of his class. In August of 1867, he made a decision to return to New England and Lowell, a burgeoning industrial city of nearly 40,000. This seemed like the ideal place to establish his fledgling practice.

Thompson built his practice into one of the largest in the city and according to an 1897 biography, worked nearly 18 hours a day, without vacation, church attendance, or other respites. Through overwork, Thompson, a vigorous man, "broke down and was obliged to build himself to vigor again." This need to restore health and vitality was how he came to invent Moxie.

A devoted teetotaler, who also forswore tobacco products of any kind, he was particularly interested in remedies and so-called cures for alcoholism. He developed a solution to addiction called the New England Cure for Alcoholism. This product achieved limited popularity and was utilized by a variety of other health professionals.

Thompson was a meticulous keeper of journals. His notes indicate that he had developed a theory which he would later expand into book form. Thompson believed that illness should be treated gradually. He also had come to the conclusion that as diseases developed from small beginnings, it was likewise logical to treat them the same way—with small doses, later progressing to larger doses. This developed from the theories prominent among other homeopathic professionals of Thompson's era. By the mid-1880s, nerve foods, of which Moxie was just one of many, had become popular with readers of newspapers and other advertising periodicals.

Moxie's growing popularity necessitated that Thompson eventually would be forced to give up his lucrative medical practice and devote himself fulltime to merchandising his nerve food.

In 1888 and early 1889, Moxie was on its way to being a prosperous product, with Thompson receiving a regular $100 per month salary. The product established extensive distribution channels, with beachheads in major urban areas like Cleveland, Ohio and George Walker's Western Moxie Nerve Food Company, in Chicago. Walker's Moxie Bottle Wagon helped make Moxie one of the most popular beverages in the American West.

As salesman fanned out over the Midwest, they often handed aluminum tokens that read, "Good for one drink of Moxie at the Moxie Bottle Wagon." These tokens had the image of the single-horse Moxie Bottle Wagon stamped on Because these tokens were quite elegant and shiny, a practice developed where young girls and older ladies would punch a hole in the token, loop a chain or decorative cord through them, and wear these coins as pendants. On the other hand, men and boys saw them as good-luck pieces, so they often ended up in drawers, instead of being handed to the Bottle Wagon drivers for a free drink of Moxie. As a result, many of these continue to be discovered and are a coveted Moxie collectible.

The Moxie Bottle Wagons traveled from town to town and were an effective advertising tool for Moxie. From an article that ran in *Yankee Magazine*, in August, 1969 titled "The Moxie Man," Edna Hills Humphrey wrote how her father, Charles E. Hills, who as a Dartmouth medical student, spent one summer vacation driving one of the Moxie Bottle Wagons around New England, "experiencing all the joys and passions of a young man out on his own."

Thompson possessed the skills of entrepreneur and his passion and creativity around promotion helped his drink's popularity rise upward. Despite the success he was seeing with the drink, he missed his medical practice and in 1889, reestablished a practice in Lowell, specializing in homeopathic medicine and surgery.

Around this time, William Taylor, an active Moxie agent in upstate New York, entered into an agreement with Thompson. Taylor's success with Moxie had allowed him to establish his own trading company, William Taylor & Company, and he became a lessee of The Moxie Nerve Food Company, within Massachusetts, taking over for Thompson. Thompson would receive $5,000 per year from this arrangement, and acquired the title of general manager of Taylor's company.

During the 1890s, William Taylor & Company added new products to their roster, such as Moxie Lozenges, Moxie Catarrh Cure, Dr. Thompson's Condensed Medicated Wafers, Moxie Syrup, and Moxie Cerealina. Moxie continued to expand westward, opening bottling operations in St. Louis and then; Kansas City, Missouri.

By 1892, a reorganization of the Moxie empire was under way. The activities of William Taylor & Co. were being curtailed and a new firm was established, at a meeting in Saco, Maine, on December 26, 1892.

The Moxie Nerve Food Company of New England was established, with offices in Boston and Lowell. Later, the Moxie Nerve Food Company of Illinois was created and operated for the next decade, before dissolving in June of 1901.

Dr. Thompson's rich and prolific life had entered its twilight. Over the last decade of his life, he continued writing plays, advertisements for Moxie, and a series of letters to newspaper editors, covering topics from geography, economics, the law, and his favorite topic—politics. Thompson became quite interested and involved in the Free Silver movement, which dominated the McKinley-Bryan presidential campaign of 1896.

Thompson continued to weigh in on subjects such as the Spanish-American War (he was in favor of swift and decisive action by the Americans) and the importance of the U.S. expanding its empire, by taking the Philippine Islands.

On November 17, 1902, Thompson sought copyright for a 114-page book, *The Origin and Continuance of Life: Together with the Development of a System of Medical Administration on the Law of the Similars, from a Discovery of its Principles in the Law of Natural Affinities.*

The book contained an illustration of a new invention, the Thompson Vitalizer, which was a contraption consisting of tanks of compressed gases, tubes, and other related apparatus. Thompson envisioned a series of parlors, up and down the east coast.

Thompson passed away, June 8, 1903, at the age of 67.

Moxie Hits The Big Time

Compared to today's ubiquitous soft drink advertising, Moxie's ground-breaking campaigns of the early 20th century were miniscule by comparison. For the time, however, Moxie was setting the standard for innovative ways to market a product.

Starting first with the horse drawn Moxie Bottle Wagons in Chicago and replicated elsewhere, the Moxie brand was being introduced to fairgoers and others, across the country.

What would become an even more effective catalyst of publicity for the burgeoning soft drink called Moxie, would be that of a series of Moxie cars. The idea, developed by Thompson's son, Francis, now president of the company his father began, included a variety of styles and makes.

Some of the cars were white Stanley Steamers and Locomobiles. Others were manufactured by Stevens-Duryea. Thompson even took regular Buicks and had them modified to be delivery trucks, with coolers mounted on the back.

In an account taken from the *Norway* (Maine) *Advertiser*, reporter Harry A. Packard describes riding around the ½ mile dirt track at the Oxford County Fair in a Moxie car. Packard had received the coveted invitation to take a spin around the track from Moxie sales agent, Lewis St. John, in the 30-horsepower Buick that served as a regional Moxie car.

"To ride in the famous Moxie automobile around the track at the annual county fair was the good fortune of this Advertiser reporter. The mile was made in the remarkable time of one minute and 44 seconds, and the greater part of the mighty speed contest was better than a mile-a-minute clip."

Obviously impressed by his ride with St. John, Packard effused further:

"For the man who has never traveled a mile a minute in a racing automobile, the brief space of a minute and 44 seconds with Mr. St. John was indeed a revelation. When one comes to consider that the Moxie automobile is heavily loaded and that the curves of the Oxford County track are very sharp for such speed, the time made was really marvelous. Sitting in the luxurious automobile at ease among the cushions, one feels practically no sensation except the whiz through space. There is no jar from the motor or engine—the old time rumble of early model machines is an unknown quantity in this 20th century marvel. Around the curves the power is shut off; then when the straight track is reached it's a mighty whiz through the air for a few seconds at fully a 75 mile a minute clip, watching the road ahead, on-on at rapid speed. A glorious ride. There in no motion or jar—it is like the graceful glide of a sled upon a smooth now clad hillside."

Throughout New England, New York, and states to the west, the Moxie automobile had a profound effect on all that had the pleasure to witness members of the Moxie mobile fleet.

Frank Archer: Moxie's Marketing Genius

As the nation's first mass-marketed soft drink, Moxie was ahead of its time. While Dr. Thompson was the drink's originator, no one was more directly responsible for its amazing popularity during the first two decades of the 20th century, than Frank Archer, Moxie's marketing genius.

Archer was hired by the Moxie Nerve Food Company of New England, in 1896. There are multiple accounts of the exact date, but the important thing was that Archer, who would be a driving force behind Moxie's popularity in the early 20th century, was now onboard the Moxie train.

Archer was born in Lincoln, Maine, August 12, 1862, the son of a doctor. The young Archer acquired his love for roaming at an early age, when he would accompany his father, a country doctor, as he made his rounds through all manner of Maine weather, visiting the sick and infirmed.

After attending public school in Bangor and working briefly in and around the Queen City, young Archer moved to Boston, where he was hired by a dry goods firm and later, an electrical company.

Archer's Moxie career began rather inauspiciously, as a soda clerk, but by 1900, Archer was heading up all Moxie advertising, overseeing two agencies and drawing a yearly salary of $4,000, a considerable sum of money at that time. Ambitious to a fault, Archer saw many possibilities for promoting the soft drink. In early 1901, Archer began utilizing billboards in large New England cities such as Boston, Providence, Lawrence, Lowell, Haverhill, and south to New York City, and even Philadelphia. These billboards, as well as cardboard signs attached to wagons, street cars, and trains read, "Don't Forget to Order Moxie."

Archer was relentless, as well as ingenuous in his promotional activities and utilized a variety of marketing devices to get the word out about Moxie. One clever ploy was taking an 1898 photograph of Theodore Roosevelt and preparing life-sized cutouts of the twenty-sixth president, with the inscription, "The Leading Exponent of a Strenuous Life." The implication was that by drinking Moxie, you could lead a strenuous, or adventuresome life just like Roosevelt, who had become a larger-than-life figure in adulthood, but who had been a sickly child.

Later, Archer would pen *The TNT Cowboy*, a fictional account of Fred, a heroic character, who like Roosevelt, had been born in the east, went west for adventure, and then moved back east. The slim pocket-size book was a reworking of the popular Horatio Alger myth, about a young boy who through hard work and perseverance, overcomes his meager beginnings, in the classic rags-to-riches saga. The traits embodied by young Fred— manliness, cleanliness, and right living—were perfect themes to build Moxie's advertising around at the time. The adventures of the TNT Cowboy found themselves interspersed throughout much of Moxie's advertising during the first two decades of the 20th century.

Archer, who worked his way up in the company, now had a platform to carry out his various ideas while promoting the soft drink.

It was Archer who came up with the Moxie Man, a character who some say favored a close resemblance to Archer himself. This image, which became synonymous with Moxie, showed up on much of the advertising material, often pointing a finger and admonishing the reader to "Drink Moxie."

Archer took full advantage of the advent of the automobile and Moxie, by building on the idea of Francis Thompson to maximize opportunities for even additional advertising for the soft drink. On February 27, 1917, Archer was granted a patent for an ornamental design of an automobile. This patent gave him carte blanche to basically ornament the chassis of any make of car he deemed appropriate, utilizing the technique described in the patent—mounting a dummy horse on the chassis, with the driver operating the particular vehicle while seated on the horse. Archer created a fleet of such vehicles and called them Moxie Horsemobiles. These became real attention-getters when they showed up at parades and fairs.

Frank Potter's *The Book of Moxie* contains a quote from Oliver Purdy on the early horses used for the Moxie Horsemobiles;

"They had a problem with the early Horsemobiles," said Purdy, who was Archer's nephew and sales manager. "Some of them were harness makers' display horses made of plaster. The vibration of the vehicle would crack them; so the drivers carried a supply of white tape to patch the cracks."

The company was able to obtain a horse from England that was made entirely of wood. The horse was mounted on a Buick chassis. This was the one that the company ended up keeping. Eventually, the company obtained a mold for $5,000 that allowed them to make perfect aluminum horses that didn't crack, or pose any problems at all.

According to an April, 1985 issue of the *Numismatist*, by the early 1950s, just one example of these original vehicles remained. A derelict Horsemobile, which was fashioned from a 1929 LaSalle roadster. Potter takes issue with claims made from people that other makes such as Packards, Cadillacs, even Pierce Arrow's were used for chassis. His point is that no record has come forth verifying this to be true.

It is thanks to Archer's tireless efforts that today Moxie is even known. When someone exhibits an uncommon degree of spirit or nerve, they are said to be full of Moxie. Without Archer, such a term or phrase may have never become prevalent.

During the 1920s, Archer's name, rather than that of any of Thompson's progeny, became synonymous with Moxie. If any mention was made of a Thompson, it was usually on Boston's society pages and was about their yachts, not New England's favorite soft drink.

The affable Archer was perfect for promotions. With his eye towards fame and fortune and frequent sightings alongside popular actors and actresses, Archer continued to seek out ways to increase Moxie's market share.

One such actor that Archer became friends with was the well-known comedian and actor from that era, Raymond Hitchcock. Hitchcock was starring in a musical comedy, called *Hitchy Koo*. Archer sought to connect Moxie with the production, by locating advertising for the soft drink in a variety of New York's newspapers, in the theater section.

Archer had been in attendance of a performance of *Hitchy Koo*, starring Hitchcock and Julie Sanderson. In one humorous scene, Sanderson pokes a lollipop in Hitchcock's face and Archer got the idea of turning out Moxie flavored treats shaped like Hitchcock.

Most of Archer's early Eureka moments ended up being moderately, to quite successful in branding Moxie. Unfortunately, the Moxie Candy Man—the lollipop molded in the image of Archer's well-known friend, Raymond Hitchcok—was not one of them. This promotion, while original and can't miss when concocted, was a source of never-ending problems.

From notations in company records, we learn that in August of 1921, twenty-eight cartons of the Candy Men were returned for rewrapping because they were sticking to the bags. Later, Archer gave the order for Bonyea Candy Company to distribute over 1,000 of the treats for free, because the company could not sell them. In the autumn of the year, a slew of Candy Men had gone soft and had to be remelted. As a result, Archer lost money on this particular promotion.

Archer had been especially proud of his Moxie Candy Man, even applying for a patent that was granted in 1922. Despite his high hopes for this promotional tool, no other products were produced beyond that initial pressing of the treat, in 1921.

While Archer's creative brain never stopped looking for ways to pitch Moxie, the main advertising vehicle, besides the Moxie Candymen, Horsemobiles, and other stunt-type advertising used for the product, was its newspaper advertising. Illustrating the old maxim that as much as things change, the more they stay the same, the common practice in Archer's day (just like our present day) was a quid pro quo strategy, with Archer (and Moxie) purchasing advertising and newspaper editors running what readers thought were news articles about the various health benefits and other topics related to Moxie. In reality, these were simply ads in disguise, or advertorials.

Around this time, Archer's son, Frank Jr. was increasingly taking an active role with the Moxie Company. With none of the Thompson relatives having the faintest interest in the soft drink business, Archer began grooming his son to succeed him.

The younger Archer, like his dad, had an eye for beautiful women and more times than not, was seen in public with one on his arm. Following in his father's footsteps, Frank Jr. became a frequent judge at various beauty contests held at New England fairs.

Storm Clouds on Moxie's Horizon

The onset of the Great Depression brought changes to the Moxie Company, primarily in the area of marketing and PR, the company's two strongest sectors. A decision was made by Moxie's board of directors, much to the chagrin of the Archers, to begin cutting back on marketing. This was a shortsighted attempt to stem costs and ride out the choppy waters of the economy's dark days. As marketing dollars were reduced, leading to a cutback on marketing throughout New England and elsewhere, this proved to be a nearly fatal mistake, as Moxie began losing market share to current soft drink behemoths, Coca-Cola and Pepsi.

An end of an era in the Moxie saga occurred when Frank Archer passed away, in April of 1937. He was 75 years-old. An argument could be made that for all intents and purposes, Archer had been Moxie for the past 50 years. In fact, there are those who would say that Moxie would be no more than a historical footnote, if not for Archer's marketing persistence, savvy, and even genius. The man who started as a lowly soda clerk, had risen to chairman of the company. Archer, who fought off imitators and counterfeiters and preserved the Moxie brand, was responsible for the term moxie being coined to represent someone with substantial spunk and toughness. With his death, things would never be the same.

After WWII, Moxie's fortunes continued downward. With reduced marketing, leading to lower sales, profits continued to erode. Layoffs began and other cost-cutting measures were introduced.

Because of war-related shortages, sugar was still scarce and soft drink bottlers were looking at ways to utilize other products as sweeteners. Moxie began experimenting with molasses (other competitors were also looking towards molasses and corn syrup). It didn't affect the taste, at least when it was first made and bottled. However, after the bottles settled during storage, or while sitting on store shelves, fermentation would occur and a yeast-like substance would form on the bottom of the bottles. The fermentation process even caused bottles to explode.

In 1949, arrangements were made with American Dry Ginger Ale Company to take over part of Moxie's business. American Dry acquired Moxie's delivery trucks and began shipping both Moxie and Pureoxia.

In 1953, in a nod to the times, sugar-free Moxie was introduced. Described as non-fattening and dietetic, the drink began being billed as "old-fashioned, mellow, full flavor." Around the same time, the formula of basic Moxie was changed, leading old-time fans to complain that Moxie no longer tasted like it used to.

The Moxie Company was now operating at a loss and talk was heard among some board members to close up shop. Despite the doom and gloom pervasive at the company's annual meeting, Purdy, now Moxie's manager of operations, noted in the annual report, in 1954 that the company's sales were about the same volume as the previous year's. This was despite a very unfavorable summer season in New England, when sales for soft drinks were down twenty-five percent across the industry.

The sales of sugar-free Moxie had been solid and Purdy thought that the new advertising program in New England had also helped the company gain some foothold, regionally. The company was also franchising bottlers in Pennsylvania to begin marketing a test product that was slightly different, but more in line with the requirements of the territory.

Beginning in 1957, Red Sox slugger Ted Williams began endorsing Moxie. The Splendid Splinter endorsed the soft drink for several years, in which he received the fee of $1,000 and stock options. The company even launched a new product, seizing on Williams' fame. Ted's Root Beer, which had been test marketed in Fitchburg, was met with enthusiasm.

In 1959, the company showed a profit of $16,637.40, the company's first profit in nearly a decade.

Moxie was acquired by Monarch-NuGrape during the mid-1960s and moved its operations to Atlanta, Georgia, home of Coca-Cola. Sales remained solid in New England and bottling remained regionally-based.

The 1970s saw a resurgence of interest in Moxie, as it neared the century mark. Collectors became interested in Moxie memorabilia of all types. Articles began appearing in a variety of publications including *Yankee. This Fabulous Century*, produced by Time-Life Books, featured Moxie. Newspapers began picking up on the interest. Author Frank Potter, wrote *The Moxie Mystique*, which would launch a new wave of interest in Moxie, the unique drink like no other.

A centennial celebration, hailing 100 years of Moxie, was held in Union, Maine, the birthplace of Moxie's founder, Dr. Augustin Thompson.

An even bigger convergence of Moxie enthusiasts, nostalgic Moxie drinkers and new converts to the cult of Moxie was just getting started, in the unlikely town of Lisbon Falls, Maine. The small community located in south central Maine was about to become worldwide headquarters for Moxie, as the brand chugged towards the 21st century.

Anicetti's House of Moxie-Lisbon Falls

Chapter 2
When Moxie Came To Town

No one knows for sure when Lisbon Falls became the hub of the Moxie universe. As with any subject lacking canonical authorization, conjecture becomes commonplace and verification of authenticity is more difficult.

When I left Maine in 1982, for greener pastures, only to return for better opportunities in 1987, the town had somehow become part of the story arc and epicenter of Moxie's unanticipated resurgence.

Oddly enough, Frank Anicetti (one of Lisbon's more colorful characters), had become the mayor of Moxietown, with his Kennebec Fruit Company (or "Kennebec's" to the locals) serving as the world headquarters of a burgeoning movement of people that genuflected at the altar of a product, whose heyday had been the early 20th century.

When I was a kid, Kennebec's was the place to go if you wanted to load up on an assortment of penny candy. Anicetti, a collector of the arcane, in the truest sense, also had acquired a reputation locally for stocking the bitter concoction, laced with gentian root, known as Moxie. As a youngster, I remember Kennebec's being jointly run by father and son, both named Frank.

The Anicetti's store has always held a timeless quality for me and many others that have ventured inside the store with yellow panels, and green trim. Entering the place from Main Street is the equivalent of modern time travel. A visitor is able to walk backwards, down that corridor of time, to an era befitting pre-WWII. The worn floor boards, the various bottles of antique Coca-Cola lining shelves near the ceiling, with hand-lettered 3 X 5 cards, inserted like flags, indicating the part of the world and time period where they were from. The vintage countertop and old-fashioned fountain, are like nothing you'd see in the 21st century. In fact, Kennebec's seemed strangely out of place, even during the early 1970s, when my friends and I used to ride our bikes downtown, to chug a mug of root beer (an Anicetti family recipe) and buy 25 cents worth of penny candy like Hot Balls, Zotz, and other chemically-enhanced and sugar-saturated candy derivatives.

The Kennebec Fruit Company, was founded by Frank's Italian immigrant grandfather, who brought his knowledge of fruit vending to America and Lisbon Falls, parlaying that skill into a successful business. Later, his father, would take over the business and eventually, young Frank fell into the business, a 75-year-old tradition, which he's continued into the new century.

While some locals cast sidelong glances when discussions originate about Anicetti and his current exalted status with Moxie aficionados from away, the popularity of his store and his own personal magnetism is obvious during each summer's annual festival celebrating the soft drink, which seems to grow every year. Now, over 20,000 people flock to Lisbon Falls the second Saturday each July, for no other reason than to watch the Moxie parade and congregate on Main Street afterwards to sample Anicetti's Moxie ice cream, watch Moxie-chuggin' contests, listen to music, and watch the fireman's muster.

Over the past couple of years, I've stopped by Kennebec's and availed myself of Anicetti's willingness to share his knowledge of local history. Each time I've stopped by, I picked up new tidbits about the town and Moxie. When I figured out I wanted to write a new book about Lisbon Falls and Moxie, I realized that it was time for a formal interview with Anicetti. My idol for collecting people's stories has always been legendary Chicago talk show host and author, Studs Terkel. Terkel's interview partner has always been the tape recorder, so if cassette tapes are good enough for him, then I decided I would visit Anicetti, armed with my $25 Radio Shack recorder and my questions.

The day I visited Anicetti's Kennebec Fruit Company, President's Day 2008, torrential rain and associated roof issues were Anicetti's order of the day. Stepping inside the historic store, I was greeted by the sound of steady drops of water falling from the classic tin punch roof, into buckets scattered about the store. The building's roof, heavy with the winter's overly abundant snow pack, was experiencing the same problems that many others were up against during this tough winter of 2007-2008.

"I'm waiting on a call from the roofer, so I hope you don't mind if I have to dump buckets from time to time," said Anicetti.

Pleased to have him give me his time for the interview, leaking roof and bucket emptying were minor intrusions, from my perch on one of the stools alongside the soda fountain.

I began by trying to get a sense of where Anicetti's passion for Moxie came from. He told me that he's drank the tonic, once considered a nerve food, as long as he could remember and that it's always been his favorite soda.

His connection to Moxie, as more than a mere connoisseur, however, began in the 1970s. His friend, Bob Labrie, from Eastern Incorporated, called to invite Frank to come to Lewiston and see his new "toy." That toy was his restored Moxie Horsemobile.

As soon as Anicetti saw this he knew that Labrie needed to be in that summer's Frontier Days Parade, so he invited him to participate. Linda Barschdorf, the local reporter for the *Lewiston Sun Journal*, wrote about the parade and snapped a picture of Labrie's Horsemobile. The photo eventually found its way to Newport News, Virginia and to one Frank Potter.

The Moxie Man's Mother, circa 1940s

Potter, an established writer, known for his knowledge of aviation and automotive history, wrote to Anicetti, inquiring about the photo that peaked his interest, particularly given his penchant for classic automobiles and other motorized novelty items, like the Horsemobile. Through correspondence with Anicetti, Potter became intrigued by the bigger story of Moxie, the drink. Drawing upon Anicetti's vast knowledge of Moxie, Potter—with preliminary information that was based upon his own research on Moxie's origins—began piecing together Moxie's story and eventually released what would become the definitive book about Moxie to that point, *The Moxie Mystique*. On the basis of that book, Potter suddenly found himself being sought and deluged by inquiries about Moxie and requests for interviews and to come and speak about Moxie. By default, Potter was now Moxie's foremost authority. With the release of *The Book of Moxie*, later, this only cemented his stature as the expert on Moxie. Anicetti became an advocate for Potter and would be the one who introduced him to Moxie fans in the Pine Tree State at a book signing in his store. This book signing would be the beginning of the phenomenon that is now the Moxie Festival in Lisbon Falls.

"The Frontier Days Festival had died out by 1979, mostly because no one wanted the task of putting it on, any more," said Anicetti. "For several years, all I heard was people complaining that the town had nothing happening after the death of Frontier days, but no one was willing to take the reins and make something happen."

Anicetti suggested to his father that they bring Potter to the store in June for a signing. His book had come out early in the year and Potter had communicated that the book was doing well. Knowing of Moxie's strong following in the area, Anicetti convinced his father that it would be good for the store.

"My father was not someone who thought very highly of marketing. When he wanted to do a promotion, however, he'd always come to me," chuckled Anicetti.

A phone call was placed to Potter and Anicetti put together a brief postcard mailing, hoping for a small turnout of Moxie fans.

"We sent out thirteen postcards I think," he recalled. "By 2:00 o'clock, when Potter arrived, we had a line outside the store."

By the time Potter had left the store 2 ½ hours later, close to five-hundred people had passed through Kennebec's store, with signed copies of *The Moxie Mystique* in hand. While this story has some of the same biblical elements of Jesus' multiplication of loaves and fishes to feed the multitudes, there was a bit more to the back story that I'll share with readers later. Still, the obvious power of Moxie was apparent and for all intents and purposes, Moxie's connection to Lisbon Falls was forged that day, courtesy of the budding friendship and mutual respect existing between Anicetti and Potter.

The two Franks: Father and Son, circa 1980

Potter would return again in 1983 for another signing and in 1984, the Androscoggin County Chamber of Commerce came forward to help organize an official event, which incorporated elements that have characterized each festival since; the chicken barbecue, what has become the state's largest parade, the fireman's muster, and, of course, the festival's main attraction, Moxie.

"The Chamber's participation can't be overemphasized," said Anicetti. "They gave the planning push that the town had been lacking."

I asked Anicetti if he ever expected the festival to take on the proportions and shape that it currently has morphed into.

"To be quite honest, I knew we had something with that first signing, but to answer your question; no. I'm amazed how big it's become."

The festival's parade, purported to be Maine's largest, attracts crowds estimated between 20,000 to 30,000 people. They come to experience a slice of Americana that is becoming increasingly difficult to find anywhere, let alone in a small Maine town, tucked away in the remote Northeast corner of the country.

"It's really quite amazing and really a positive thing," he added. "When you see a kid outside, six, seven-years-old, sitting down in front, sharing with a senior citizen what Moxie means to them, it shows the power of Moxie to bring people together."

Anicetti, who was born in 1940, has seen the town change dramatically. We talked a bit about how the Lisbon Falls of his youth and the town I remember growing up in during the late 1960 and early 70s, had changed less during that span of time than the subsequent changes that have occurred since I was a child in town.

I asked Anicetti to talk about the things he remembered from his youth about the town and how it has changed into the place we know today.

"When you walked down Main Street, you'd stop and talk to everybody. There were the typical street people you'd find in many other places; Benny McGraw, Mary Dumas and everyone remembers Clamfoot."

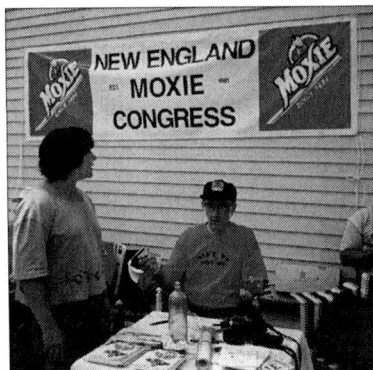

Frank Potter outside Kennebec's, 2004

After my interview with Anicetti, I wanted to do some additional fact-checking. The story, as told by The Moxie Man, appears to be pretty close to the official story, given that much of the information about Moxie is in the hands of a small inner circle of people. Still, by talking to several various sources, I'm sticking with Anicetti's narrative, with one minor addition.

I never quite bought the idea that you can send out thirteen postcards, as Anicetti swears by, and end up with a mob of five-hundred Moxie fans. I know that the drink has a rabid following (some would call this a cult following), but this story, as is, was just a little too tough for me to swallow. In fact, there is a bit more about Potter's book that readers need to know, so as promised earlier, here it is:

Potter, who was born in New England, in Massachusetts, was an established writer, with a vast array of writing credits to his name. With the release of *The Moxie Mystique*, a number of media outlets became interested in his subject matter. One of those outlets, *ABC's Today Show*, had Mr. Potter on as a guest in March, 1982.

The day prior to Potter's signing at Kennebec's, he had been on a local talk show, hosted by *WKXA*, in Brunswick, where he held court for three hours about all things Moxie, discussing upcoming signings and taking calls from listeners.

Of course, Anicetti's thirteen postcards and word of mouth generated buzz locally. Multiplied by the *WKXA* call-in slot and then, an article in the *Brunswick Times Record*, word about Potter's appearance began to spread like a small wildfire in the nation of Moxie.

When Potter returned to Kennebec's in 1983, three TV crews showed up for the second annual Moxie party. One group at the Lisbon Falls party, Muriel Heath, from Union Maine, Dr. Augustin Thompson's hometown, decided to designate Moxie Days for July 13th and 14th, the following year. The 13th would take place in Lisbon Falls and the 14th would take place in Union, to commemorate the 100th anniversary of Moxie.

As I concluded my interview with Anicetti, there was one last item I wanted to get to the bottom of. Given that Lisbon's annual summer festival is hailing 2008 as "Moxie Goes Silver," touting this summer as their 25th consecutive year, something about the math didn't add up, particularly since Anicetti is using the first Potter signing in 1982 as the start of what we know as the festival, today. Amidst speculation about dates and timelines concerning the festival, here's how we arrive at this important milestone commemorating Lisbon's 25 years partnered with Moxie.

First, if you take the original Anicetti/Potter signing as Moxie's commencement in the town of Lisbon, this makes 2008 the 26th year of the festival. Utilizing 1984 as a possible start date, which could be done, as this was the year when the Androscoggin County Chamber of Commerce became a partner, then 2008 would be the 24th year of continuous festivities.

Per usual, Anicetti lent clarity to it all with an explanation that works for me and gives a sense of the grassroots nature of how the festival happens each and every year.

"If we take Potter's first signing as the start, which is what I use, then this is our 26th year. The festival committee uses The Chamber's involvement as the beginning of what they consider the start of the official Moxie Festival. That makes 2008, twenty-four years. We decided to split the difference and call it twenty-five," said Anicetti.

Hence, 2008 is the 25th anniversary of the Moxie Festival. It's the official Silver Anniversary and with that, "Moxie Goes Silver" makes perfect sense.

From these humble beginnings, people now stream into Lisbon Falls each July, not just from Maine, or the other forty-nine states, but from all over the world, drawn to the celebration of an old-time soft drink, coming for the nostalgia that it evokes, the togetherness and civic engagement on display, and for an old-fashioned festival that is short on high tech glitz and long on the richness of community.

If Frank Anicetti is the "Moxie Man" behind Lisbon's Moxie Festival, providing a happy, gregarious face for the media and throngs of fans pulled in by Dr. Thompson's unique drink, then Sue Conroy is the behind-the-scenes maven that helps bring all the necessary and divergent logistics together each year, to make one of Maine's largest summer festivals, possible.

Conroy brought her young family to Lisbon Falls, two years after the first Potter book signing. She was attracted to the community's small town ambience. Like the many attendees, from town and from away, who come to participate in the festivities the second Saturday, every July, she was unaware of all that went into making it happen.

A local hair stylist, working out of her daughter's shop, located in the heart of downtown Lisbon Falls, she was privy to rumors and rumblings that the two local businessmen who headed up the small committee that made the festival happen were looking to get done. Both Noyes Lawrence and Dick Laroche, had been key players in putting together Lisbon's major annual event, for the past several years. Without anyone to step in and take the reins, there was a good possibility that the festival would die out.

Conroy's fortuitous step forward almost didn't happen. Twice she left messages indicating her desire to participate and no one followed up with her.

"I was at a Green Thumb meeting (a local beautification group) in 1999 and Noyes (Lawrence) was asking if anyone was interested in taking over for him in heading up the Moxie committee, as he was going to be stepping down," said Conroy. "I said 'yeah,' but I've tried to volunteer twice already and no one's called me back."

Lawrence called her back and she asked what kind of time commitment was required.

"Noyes told me 'just a few hours a week,'" laughed Conroy, now knowing how much he wanted out.

She spent time between April and the festival in July, following Lawrence around "like a puppy dog," learning what he did and making notes on what she'd do the following year, if she decided to assume his role.

"I continued to shadow Noyes during the festival follow-up. He handed me four boxes of stuff (notes and paperwork)," said Conroy. "When I asked him about the budget and all these other details, he told me that he'd be available, which he was."

Conroy was complimentary about how Lawrence helped her transition, by introducing her to as many people as possible, letting them know that she was taking over.

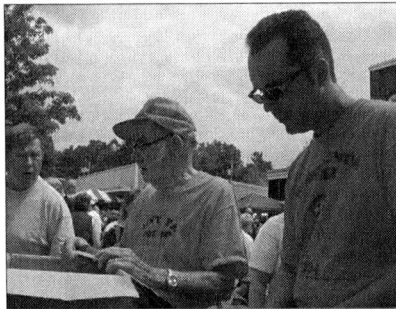

The author meets Potter for the first time, 2004

"He made himself available by phone and regularly checked in with me. He had done it for six, or seven years and while he was great in helping me with the ropes, he was ready to be done."

Beginning in 2000, Conroy was on her own. While Lawrence was a phone call away, it was now her show. Like any volunteer, no one notices when things go right, only when something goes wrong.

"I just learned by trial and error. I've gotten yelled at," she said, "I got yelled at on stage by someone that was just slightly irate. I got yelled at by a group of people who didn't get what they thought they should have. This was my first year. I've gotten yelled at a few times since then."

Conroy's experiences with Moxie have helped her arrive at a philosophical approach to her role and the responsibilities of shepherding the small band of energetic volunteers that make things happen.

"We're a small group of volunteers," she acknowledges.

"We have a small committee. We do what we can. We're all volunteers and volunteers do no wrong." That attitude has served Conroy well, over the past eight years.

In 2004, I joined the group, at her suggestion and became the festival's marketing and PR person, as well as fellow volunteer. Expecting a much larger group, particularly having witnessed numerous festivals as a spectator, I was shocked to find only seven or eight people at my initial meeting, in February, 2004.

The experience of helping to be part of planning and executing that year's festival, as well as the next year in 2005 (while also writing and publishing my first book) helped me appreciate the work that Conroy and her crew perform.

While it's always easy to be a critic, volunteers like Conroy give back so much more than they take from their communities. Year after year, tens of thousands of visitors stream into Lisbon to partake of the parade on Saturday, as well as other activities around town.

Quick to defer recognition and reluctant to revel in the spotlight, Conroy already begins planning the next year's festival, often while sitting on the judges stand, downtown, during the parade.

"On Moxie day, I'm looking at groups that are there, with an eye towards what works and what doesn't. I'll be making judgements; 'no,' you're not worth what we paid you, or, 'yes,' I want this person or group back. I then take that list and that's what I work off, scheduling for the following year's festival."

Conroy's leadership has taken the festival to new heights of popularity and recognition. Never content to rest on her laurels, she's constantly tweaking, adding new elements, trying to top the previous year's success. With the bar being raised each and every year, it becomes increasingly tough to top what's gone on in past years. Conroy and Anicetti now regularly field requests from national media outlets, often starting in March, or April, in anticipation for July. The wildly popular *Food Network* has covered the festival twice over the past couple of years.

At one time the festival was pretty much a one day event. Saturday's parade, the fireman's muster, and, of course, Moxie ice cream at Kennebec's, the festivities were usually over by 2:30.

Only volunteers and the street sweeper left as a reminder of the event. Under Conroy's care, the festival now lasts all weekend, beginning with a full Friday night slate. In 2004, a family street carnival, spearheaded by the local fire company was added, pulling families, with children to the blocked off downtown area. The year after that fireworks were added to make the perfect late night set up and precursor for Saturday's festivities. Add Sunday's well-attended canoe race on the Androscoggin and Moxie has become a true festival and a destination event.

Line begins forming at House of Moxie,
for Moxie Ice Cream

"In the past, if you came downtown at 4:00 o'clock, you could walk down the street and outside of few flyers rolling around, there was an empty stage and no Moxie. Now, it's pretty well the weekend. We still have a lot of out-of-towners who stop on Sunday to see Frank (Anicetti) and say, 'Where's the Moxie Festival?' But I can't get anybody to agree to make it a whole weekend downtown where we set up and stay set up. That's fine with me. I think it's big enough as it is. I don't want us to lose sight of the fact that Moxie is a down home festival and I think that's what attracts many of the visitors to town. We're still the only festival in the world that celebrates a soda," adds Conroy.

So why Lisbon Falls and Moxie? Conroy credits Anicetti as the catalyst that brought Moxie and Lisbon Falls together. The odd partnering, of a strange-tasting soft drink, invented by a Mainer—but not someone from town—and its emergence twenty-five years ago, as the Moxie Mecca seems quite improbable. Never underestimate the passion that people bring to their interests and hobbies, however.

"Frank's book signing is what made it all happen," said Conroy. "He became the Moxie Man and his store is the Moxie Store. A couple of Moxie aficionados turned Lisbon Falls into Moxie Town."

I often wonder what happens to Lisbon's role with Moxie in five, or ten years from now. From my perspective, as someone who grew up in town, knows the community, as well as having served alongside both Conroy and gotten to know Anicetti, I'm doubtful that without one, or both of them, Moxie continues to be the focal point of the town's summer.

At the end of the interview I conducted with Conroy, I asked her about this. Her answer was in line with how I've always perceived her to be—honest, hard-working and quick to give credit to those who deserve it.

"I don't plan on doing this job forever. People ask every year, 'are you going to do it again; are you going to do it again?' I've said if someone wants to take over, I'll be glad to show them how and I'll still stay involved, but right now, there is no one to take over. I think it's going to be one of those hit-or-miss things, like what happened between Noyes and I, when I stepped forward."

Conroy's more concerned about Anicetti's departure.

"I'm not worried about when I quit. I'm worried about when Frank quits."

Taurus the Clown at Moxie, 2005

Maine humorist, Gary Crocker, in Jackman, Maine

Chapter 3

Moxie Becomes Law

State of Maine

———

IN THE YEAR OF OUR LORD
TWO THOUSAND AND FIVE

———

S.P. 27 – L.D. 85

An Act To Establish Moxie as Maine's Official Soft Drink
Be it enacted by the People of the State of Maine as follows
Sec. 1. 1 MRSA §224 is enacted to read:
§224. State soft drink

Moxie, a registered trademarked soft drink invented by Maine-born Dr. Augustin Thompson of Union that symbolizes spirit and courage, is the official state soft drink.

In the 1930s, pre-New Deal Republican politicians claimed, "As Maine Goes, So Goes The Nation." Dirigo, our state motto means, "I Lead." I suppose it's fitting that on May 21, 2005, we became the first and only state in the union to name an official state soft drink.

The genesis of the idea to have Moxie recognized officially, by state law, came from a group that included Fred Goldrup, from Lewiston, State Senator, Peggy Rotundo (D-Lewiston) who sponsored the legislation, Frank "Moxie Man" Anicetti and Maine humorist and lifetime member of the New England Moxie Congress, Gary Crocker. Also in attendance were several other NEMC members.

Mainers have always had moxie—a certain spunk, toughness and can-do spirit—by signing the bill, Governor Baldacci (with a handful of pens courtesy of Anicetti) made it official. Mainers now had an official soft drink to rightfully match their character.

It was Crocker, who back in March of 2005, spoke before the Joint Standing Committee on State and Local Government and delivered a manifesto of sorts, in support of Moxie being granted special status by the state and ultimately being recognized as the state's official drink.

"Senator Schneider, Representative Barstow, distinguished members of the Joint Standing Committee on State and Local Government; I am Gary Crocker, a Maine native and life member of the New England Moxie Congress. I live on a dirt road in West Gardiner, Maine, but travel around the county making remarks based on the magic of our great state and the people who live here. Among our assets are special and unique qualities of character, commitment, and rock solid resolve to getting the job done—no matter what it takes. We even invented Moxie originally patented as a nerve food capable of curing multiple maladies! Since 1884 the term Moxie has come to be part of our lexicon and representative of the spirit of our great state and some say, our nation. It has been used by statesmen, actors, business leaders and even Maine humorists to make a simple but important point, we've got what it takes to get the job done—we've got nerve!

So—how did Moxie come to mean what it does? And why is it forever connected to our great state? Very simply, the basic meaning of the word (moxie) was born when Dr. Augustin Thompson's Moxie Nerve Food began to push its way past the palates of the populace. Thereafter, whenever anyone exhibited an uncommon amount of nerve, that person is said to "have moxie."

This bill presents us with an almost mystical opportunity to connect our great state with the application of a word that makes a powerful and positive statement each and every time it is uttered. It all started here in Maine in 1884; let's make it official by making Moxie our official state beverage and forever establishing Maine as not only having moxie but inventing both the soft drink and the phrase!

I urge the committee to vote unanimous, "Ought to pass" on LD 85.

Thank you for the opportunity to address the committee. I would be happy to address any questions you may have."

While other efforts no doubt helped to push LD 85 across the finish line towards passage, Crocker's passionate and eloquent explanation to the Joint Standing Committee on State and Local Government certainly was instrumental in the bill's passage and being signed into law.

Newspaper accounts that accompanied the bill's signing indicated that the governor has been a supporter of Moxie. Every second Saturday in July, you'll be sure to find Baldacci, in Lisbon Falls, riding in the state's largest annual parade. Later, he makes his way back behind the counter, at Anicetti's Kennebec Fruit Company, ice cream scoop in hand, dipping out cones and fixing Moxie floats for surprised out of towners. Baldacci, who grew up in a restaurant family, which ran (and still runs) Momma Baldacci's, in Bangor, knows all about the food business and what it takes.

More than just a politically-motivated gesture, Baldacci's signing the bill stems from his own passion for the drink.

The governor stated to members of the press at the time of the signing, "I am a Moxie drinker. I do the Moxie Festival every year," he said.

Another important person in making Moxie the official drink of Maine was Fred Goldrup. Goldrup ended up being the initial catalyst behind the bill's ultimate passage and signing. Someone with more than just a passing interest in Moxie, Goldrup has played Taurus the Clown since the first Moxie Festival parade, in 1984. He is also a lifetime Moxie drinker and aficionado, as well as a member of the NEMC. Senator Rotundo's constituent, he went to the senator, to see if she would sponsor the bill.

According to Goldrup, Maine was without a state beverage at the time. Other states have given recognition to a particular drink—cranberry juice in Massachusetts, orange juice in Florida, milk in New York—why not Moxie in Maine? In fact, Goldrup had been thinking about this for several years, considering why this was and how Moxie would be the perfect antidote to this problem.

Because Goldrup was born with a hearing impairment (having fifteen percent hearing in his left ear and totally deaf in his right), phone interviews, or even in-person tape recorded sessions wouldn't work. Fortunately for me (and readers), Goldrup, at age seventy-four, is tech savvy and comfortable with email. His thoughts about the bill came via several lengthy email exchanges between us. I have included them as he sent them, because they capture the passion that Moxie drinkers have about their drink.

Well, Maine did not have a State Beverage. I thought of this for several years, actually. I wrote the Bill to name MOXIE "the official drink of Maine". I read that Connecticut (or was it Rhode Island?) had coffee milk for their official beverage. I know of a few Mainers who make home brew. Quite a few years ago, there was a firm in Maine that created a Vodka (Cold River Vodka, in Freeport-JB) from potatoes. Neither one, in my opinion, should have that honor of being Maine's official beverage. You are aware of what the word, "MOXIE", means, so I won't get into that. I wrote my State Senator, Peggy Rotundo, about how the MOXIE definition defined the Mainer. I knew the inventor was born in Union and migrated to some state somewhere South of L.L.

Bean. It was there, he created this elixir of the Gods.

Maine (as Frank Anicetti would tell you) was THE site of the FIRST tossing of tea from England's cargo ship in protest of the "tea tax". It moved down the Coast where it hit Boston. Of course, Maine was PART of Massachusetts at the time, but it is MY opinion that the history books were often wrong in reporting things. Be that as it may, I felt Maine needed an official drink, and so, MOXIE came to mind. I wrote Senator Rotundo of my thoughts (a nine or 10-page letter). I was pleased she liked the idea. I had submitted it too late to include in 2004's Legislation debates, so Senator Rotundo suggested I wait and she'd submit it for the following year.

I had been approached by people telling me dairy farmers and Poland Spring Water might object and campaign against MOXIE as the official beverage, they suggested I change my bill to name MOXIE as the official SOFT drink. The thought of the Poland Spring Water had occurred to me. Rather than have the Bill shot down and shelved for a few years, I agreed to the change.

No one was more surprised than I when the Committee decided to pass the Bill right then at the first hearing, rather than submit the Bill to the Legislature.

"Fred's a great guy and a real aficionado for Moxie," said Senator Rotundo.

Rotundo, who has served in the Senate since 2000 and is the Chair of the Senate's Appropriations Committee, which oversees the state's 6.3 billion dollar biennial budget. As such, she was the perfect choice to champion the legislation.

Rotundo introduced the legislation and then elicited support from a colleague, Robert Berube (R-Lisbon). Berube and Rotundo represent different ends of the political spectrum, but Moxie pulled these two together, proving that Moxie might be more than just a cure for what ails you, physically. It might also be an elixir promoting bipartisanship among politicians.

"I wanted to have Bob as one of the sponsors, since he's from the area (Lisbon)," said Rotundo.

Asked about how the introduction of a bill recognizing Moxie was met by her fellow members of the senate.

"I got a lot of ribbing for it," admitted Rotundo. "I've always been a serious legislator, so my colleagues enjoyed letting me know about that, when I introduced the Moxie bill In fact, Gary Crocker, the Maine humorist, said I was 'the perfect person' to sponsor the bill, because people would take it serious."

Despite the good-natured ribbing that accompanied running legislative interference on Moxie's behalf, Rotundo says she's proud that she was behind getting Moxie official recognition.

"I'm very proud to be the sponsor," said Rotundo. "I think Moxie symbolizes something much larger for the people of Maine and New England."

According to Rotundo, she believes the bill's introduction and the surrounding publicity that accompanied it and the actual signing has been good for Maine.

"The process created an enormous amount of interest both statewide and nationally, for Maine," said Rotundo.

When asked about the signing ceremony with the governor,

Rotundo had this to say.

"I've never seen so much orange in one place," she said. "We had people from throughout New England at the ceremony. To this day, I still have the original can of Moxie I was presented at the signing, in my office [at Bates College]."

The final passage of the bill, while hailed by fans of Moxie, did elicit a rash of Letters to the Editor, criticizing the legislature, for taking time from more important work, to crown Moxie, as the state's official soft drink. And it turned out it was necessary to label Moxie the state's "official soft drink, rather than the state's 'official drink,' as the original bill stipulated. This would have irked the Maine dairy industry and would have led their lobbyists to raise concern.

Regardless of a few naysayers—as Crocker, Anicetti, and Goldrup will attest—having the state recognize Moxie is a good thing, because Mainers certainly have moxie!

Chapter 4
Stories of Moxie

<u>Lara Tupper/Writer</u>

Lara is a wonderful writer, who also happens to hail from lovely Boothbay Harbor, Maine. We met at a book signing for her first novel, *One Thousand and One Nights*, based upon her own experiences as an entertainer, aboard cruise ships. She sends her Moxie story, which took place at Moody's Diner, in Waldoboro.

The last time I had a can was at Moody's Diner in August 2007. It was kept in a small fridge in the gift shop and sold as other "Maine" tidbits might be—as a keepsake. In the company of balsam pillows and AYUH bumper stickers, the Moxie can seems iconic: the cure for the northern sweet-tooth. I suppose a can from Moody's is something to wash out and display, proof that you've been there once you're not there anymore. Which is a little weird, I think. Like keeping a candy bar wrapper just because you liked the taste or because the colors are cool. The Moxie colors are Halloween-y, which seems right. (A friend from Bangor, now living close to me in NYC, has a badass Moxie tattoo on her arm.) The taste of Moxie is scary in a Halloween way too. There's something metallic and hard there, something a little ghoulish. You feel tough getting it down.

You might wonder what I was doing in Moody's in the height of the tourist season and this is a very good question. My Mom had bought perennials from a nearby gardening shop and had pulled into the crowded parking lot on a whim. We happened to run into my cousin and her husband there—all of us apparently in need of pie that afternoon. But it felt a little preordained. We'd stopped by chance and left with family news and too much sugar on our teeth. And then I bought more sugar in the gift shop. I didn't keep my Moxie can but I thought about it. That's what happens when you stay away from Maine too long.

Tess Gerritsen/Best selling author

Gerritsen is a best selling author, who happens to live in Camden. A regular on the New York Times Best Seller List, with her medical thriller novels and tales of detective, Jane Mazzioli, Gerritsen is surprisingly accessible, regularly answering emails.

I decided to inquire about her knowledge of Moxie and sought a possible or story, or anecdote from her. Her first email went as follows:

Hi Jim,

Thanks for writing! While I'm certainly familiar with Moxie and its history, I'm afraid I've never actually sampled the product. It's hard to find in my local store!

Tess

We swapped emails, as I indicated she should be able to find it at her local Hannaford Supermarket. I inquired about an upcoming appearance she was making in Lewiston. She wrote back that she would try to locate it.

Not one to miss an opportunity to do something different, I decided to pick up a six-pack of Moxie and present it to her after her talk, in Lewiston, at the Public Library.

She was surprised and I wish I had brought a camera and had someone capture the moment. Here is her response when I wrote to inquire if she had found an opportunity to try Moxie.

Jim,

Thanks for the introduction to Moxie! My husband and i both cracked open a can that evening and it reminded us a lot of root beer ... and yet, with an extra taste that i think might have been star anise? Vaguely Asian, in fact, and I'm wondering if anyone ever uses Moxie to cook with. Say, to make an Asian-type marinade for barbecue or something. Quite unique, and not at all weird!

tess

Mark LaFlamme/Horror writer and reporter at the Lewiston Sun Journal

You have to read Mark LaFlamme, to really appreciate him. He's been with the paper since the mid-90s, beginning as a beat reporter. He's also branched out and written a Stephen King-esque horror novel called, *The Pink Room*, as well as *Asterisk*, a book about baseball and "how the game will be played in 2086 and how the Red Sox will fare as knowledge and progress rocket humankind into the future." His experience follows:

When I was a boy, my mother talked about her experiences with Moxie and as a result, I never developed a taste for the beverage. In fact, I have an aversion to the drink the way some will develop an aversion to medicines that haunted them in youth.

As the story goes, my mother had what was diagnosed as an iron deficiency (found out in a later email that it was anemia) when she was a child growing up on a farm in Oakland, Maine. To boost her iron levels, she was prescribed Moxie with raw liver, taken together. Her description of those flavors when together was horrid and as a result, I steered toward RC Cola instead of Moxie. Plus, you could win cash money by scraping off the underside of the cap when RC.

Probably not the fond Moxie memory you were looking for.

LaFlamme emailed me back to say that the condition that his mother suffered from, warranting the Moxie prescription, was anemia.

Carol Noonan/Maine singer-songwriter and owner of the Stone Mountain Arts Center

Carol is an incredible talent and her Stone Mountain Arts Center, tucked in the heart of Maine's western mountains is not to be missed. Carol is a talented writer in her own right, penning the evocatively funny *Dear Mr Was…Letters from Maine*. She contributed the following Moxie memory of Moxie, bad eyesight and the drink's "medicinal" qualities, and sibling love:

When we were kids, my parents would go out at least one of the weekend nights. It was the only time we got soda or coke as we referred to everything, whether it was orange or root beer. Anyway, my mom's eyes were starting to go, as mine are now, when she was in her fifties. She started bringing home things she didn't mean to buy from the store. Usually it was a diet version of something, that was right next to the original. Ya see where this is going? Yes, not only did she buy us Moxie for our big Friday night without the parents, but she got diet moxie!!!! We assumed she was goin' for the root beer....there was a brand with an orange label. But Moxie with our fondue...and diet no less??? We were devastated...but just desperate enough for something bubbly that we tried it. It was simply and utterly "medicine." My Dad had been drinking "medicine" all these years with his cheezits and we sure as hell were not going to be the generation that passed along that tradition without sugar. We opted for our tried and true back up plan.....the Nestles Quick, blended with some ice...a sad replacement for an icy cold classic coke in the bottle, with a bendy flexy straw. Anyway, it was a night I will always remember......*also my brother locked me in the closet and forgot about me.*

Bill Green/*WCSH* host of "Bill Green's Maine"

Bill Green is a reporter who regularly chronicles the unique aspects of what makes Maine a special place to live, as well as visit. Green, who grew up in Bangor, had his own tale about Moxie that he graciously shared with me.

I was about six years old. The baseball game was always in my backyard. The sun is setting on a beautiful summer evening. My dad drives in and surveys the scene. As the game winds down, Dad suggests we all go for a Moxie. We pile into the old car and head down to Ken Day's Store. Dad comes out with six ice cold Moxies. "This is what we drank when I was a kid," he said as he passed out the bottles. We all took a swig and started gagging. "This is awful!" "Yuk!" Our implied thought was, "You ruined our game for this?"

Every so often I have a Moxie just to remember my dad. I don't really like the taste to this day! I don't know if you can use this, but I always think of Moxie with a smile.

Kent Ward/Longtime columnist for *Bangor Daily News*

Kent wrote one of the best reviews that were done for *When Towns Had Teams*. He captured the sociological thread running through the book. A longtime Mainer, as well as a journalist, I welcomed his recollection about a "fight" with Moxie and its potential as a weapon.

Good to hear from you again. Moxie was one of my favorite soft drinks when I was a kid. I find that today, however, I can take it or leave it. I have a can of it in my fridge from a couple of years ago, left there by a grand-nephew, an Army helicopter pilot, when he was home on leave. He loves the stuff, but, being stationed down South (Ft.

Rucker, Alabama) he can't get it. Various family members send him some from time to time, and he always gets a supply for Christmas.

I don't have any particular memories that might be worthy of inclusion in your book. Unless you count the time that my younger brother and I got into a Moxie fight at the little country crossroads store that once stood on my property here in Limestone. It was in the 1940's. We were perhaps ages 11 and 9, and like the rest of the neighborhood kids, used to walk the mile or so to the store for penny candy when we had the pennies to spend.

One day after we each had bought a bottle of Moxie we got to shaking it and—thumbs partially covering the neck of the bottle— squirting the concoction at each other, as kids will do. The thing is, we were inside the store at the time and made quite the sticky mess.

The kindly old proprietor kicked us out and we were so ashamed of the episode—and so afraid that he would tell our parents—that we made ourselves scarce the rest of the summer. Fortunately for us, he never did rat us out. But when a parent subsequently would send one of us to the store for sugar, or molasses, or whatever, we always conned a neighborhood buddy into entering the store and making the purchase while we remained outside and attempted to stay out of sight.

Eventually, the store owner grew concerned about our absence and sent word by the other kids that all was forgiven and he hoped he'd soon be seeing us again. I don't know whether Moxie is good for removing the rust from car bumpers, and what-not, as some of the other popular soft drinks were (are) rumored to be. But I can assure you that, properly shaken and poorly aimed in a spirited duel between rambunctious lads of summer, it can become a weapon that sure can land a kid in trouble.

Best wishes. And good luck with your book.

Kent

Gary Crocker/Maine humorist (Lifetime member, NEMC)

Gary's humor is well-known in these parts. A regular attendee and frequent performer at the annual Moxie Festival, Gary spoke eloquently in support of the bill that made Moxie the "official soft drink of Maine."

I am a true Moxie lover and you will ALWAYS find ice cold Moxie in my refrigerator. Stop by anytime and see for yourself!

I was "taught" to drink Moxie by my grandfather, Russell Cram of North Monmouth. I say "taught" because as you know, Moxie is an acquired taste and cannot possibly be appreciated in a single sitting especially if it is your first encounter with Maine's official soft drink (signed into law by Governor John Baldacci on May 20, 2005). I was at the signing along with other bill supporters as reported in the Lewiston Sun Journal on Saturday May 21, 2005.

I often comment on the unusual taste of Moxie at my performances and do my best to prepare them for their first encounter with this marvelous drink laced with Gentian Root Extractives. I don't want them to be put off at their first attempt so I warn them that it tastes a little bit like root beer..........that's gone WICKED BAD!!!!!!!! And if that's not enough, I tell them that if they are having a party at their place and they are expecting six friends and they want to be sure each guest has at least one can of soft drink they should get a six pack of Moxie. They might force one down, but they're NOT going to ask for another one!

By the way, don't try the Moxie energy drink. It tastes nothing like Moxie, it tastes good. Just like all those other energy drinks which is just the point. Moxie is unique and stands alone in the Cola wars. It never goes on sale like other sodas because if you like it you'll pay whatever it costs to get your hands on a can, and if you haven't acquired a taste for it you wouldn't drink it if we gave it to you. Which is why I always kept Moxie in the refrigerator when the kids were growing up. I knew I would always have a soft drink when I needed one because the kids wouldn't touch it.

Thank you grampa Cram for teaching me to drink Moxie. It is more than a soft drink. It is a statement about who we are here in the State of Maine.

And the name is used around the globe to indicate that someone has guts or hutzpa. I think that says it all. Dr. Augustin Thompson from Union Maine started something when he introduced Moxie Nerve Tonic onto the market and we continue to reap the benefits to this day. I think I'll take a break and have a Moxie right now dontcha know mister man!

Ayuh

Margaret Evans Porter/Historical novelist, blogger and also, State Representative for Merrimack County, New Hampshire (District 8)

Margaret maintains the lovely *Periodic Pearls* blog, where she writes about her life as a writer, alternating between Great Britain and New Hampshire. The author of 11 period novels, she shared a Moxie story of her own, about being introduced to the drink.

Jim,

Great to hear from you!

I'd heard of Moxie before coming to New England. My husband's dad's family is from Danver/Salem MA and his grandmother's family, the Hamlins, are from Otisfield in Maine.

Drinking my first Moxie occurred on my very first trip to New England, for our honeymoon, and it was a necessary ritual. Seriously. This was many years before I came to New England to live. I'm afraid I didn't exactly join the cult as a result. We often found Moxie in the fridge when my father-in-law had been to stay at the cottage. (Because he lives in North Carolina now, where it's not available!)

Margaret

John Lehaney/Retired Community College Counselor (NEMC historian)

John sends this piece from Missouri, where he and his wife now reside. The former New Englander (from Leominster, MA) titled his note, "Appreciating Moxie," which captures some of the nostalgia of the drink, particularly the old drugstore soda fountains, where John reports, a soda clerk "custom made" your drink of Moxie.

My appreciation of Moxie started in the 1930's. That was a time when a fortunate child could be taken to a drugstore for penny candy or to sit at the soda fountain for a bigger treat. For teenage boys the best soda fountain was also the best place to meet friends and talk about sports, movies, music and girls. Ancient comic books report this era with Harold Teen and the Sugar Bowl Soda Shop.

Five cent fountain drinks were appealing. They were custom made by the clerk who first shot syrup into a glass up to the fill line, then injected a stream of carbonated water, and then gave it a short stir with a spoon. If the soda clerk was a friend, the syrup could go a bit above the line. You could mix the flavors. Some never had a straight Coke. Cherry Coke, vanilla Coke and chocolate Coke were popular.

The different drink was Moxie, not as sweet as other drinks, and some did not like it at all. For a thirsty minority, Moxie was the drink of choice. You could mix it with other flavors, but most Moxie drinkers took it straight. Moxie's advertising promoted its exclusive qualities with statements such as "Never sticky sweet, Distinctively different, If at all particular, A unique taste, Healthful, and Learn to enjoy Moxie."

It was like nothing else, and it still is, and this drinker still appreciates it.

Along the way of collecting stories, I also found some interesting uses of Moxie that I didn't know about, namely, as a mixer. Here is a list of drinks that was passed along. Please keep in mind that I didn't come up with these names, I merely report for your edification.

Notable Moxie mixed drinks include the "Welfare Mom", which consists of equal parts Diet Moxie and Allen's Coffee Flavored Brandy the "County Girl", a drink made up of one part Bourbon Whiskey and two parts Moxie on the rocks, with an optional lime garnish; the "Mad Mailman", a mixture of Moxie and Jagermeister; and "The Vijay", which consists of one part Moxie and one part blended American Whiskey. Many people, even those who do not like the soda on its own, find it refreshing when mixed with whiskey.

Colin Woodard/Writer

Colin hails from the western mountains of Maine. He is an author, as well as an award-winning journalist, who writes regularly for *The Christian Science Monitor*, as well as *The Chronicle of Higher Education.* He is the author of several books, including *The Lobster Coast: Rebels, Rusticators and the Struggle for a Forgotten Frontier*, in my opinion, one of the most accurate books about Maine that dispels many of the myths about the state.

Colin and I traded emails and he sent me the following story about Moxie.

When I was a kid in western Maine in the late seventies, I had no idea that Moxie had been invented in our state. It seemed a bit anachronistic, with that guy in the white labcoat pointing at you like Uncle Sam's brother, the government weapons scientist ("I want YOU to frighten Stalin by inventing the hydrogen bomb!") In my small town, it was a drink popular with the older generation, like saspirilla or birch beer. We elementary school kids watched plenty of television and so were already loyal to Coke, Pepsi, and 7-Up.

One afternoon after a Farm Team baseball practice, I went out on a limb and spent my precious snack money on a can of Moxie. I hated it: not enough of that high fructose corn syrupy goodness. But as I approach middle age, I actually like it: not too sweet and with a mildly objectionable aftertaste that makes you want to try another sip. ("That can't be right. Let's try that again.") It reminds me a lot of Kofola, a soft drink invented by the Czechoslovak Communist Party as a Socialist alternative to Coke and Pepsi, which now outsells both in Slovakia. Did some Mainer pass Moxie's secrets to the enemy?

Chapter 5

The Homecoming: Moxie Makes Its Way Back To New England

By the mid-1960s, the Moxie brand was in trouble. The drink's heyday was long past. Attempts at reviving the drink, utilizing advertising with New England icons, like Ted Williams, proved ineffective. Launches of new products did little to make a dent in the market share of giants like Coke and Pepsi, even on a regional basis. Similar regional off-brands like Dr. Pepper, had achieved national market penetration. Moxie languished.

The Moxie Company, now based in Needham Heights, Massachusetts, was forced to dissolve its operations. Moxie had become nothing more than a nostalgic brand, without a marketing strategy and little power to compete in the highly competitive soft drink world of the day.

When Monarch Beverages Company acquired the brand Moxie, in 1966, it was part of an initial strategy that the company had taken on to build a stable of nostalgic sodas, similar to Moxie. Later, Monarch acquired the National NuGrape Company, and by consolidating various small niche companies, certain economies of scale were developed. As a result, this provided cash flow to expand brands like Moxie. Unfortunately, the strategy also included dubious new products, such as vitamins, dairy ingredients and bubble gum.

Monarch Beverage Company, based in Atlanta was founded in 1965, by Frank Armstrong, an advertising executive who had spent years working with a international brands and clients. Armstrong's experience had supplied him with awareness about the untapped potential of smaller, regional soft drinks, each one coming equipped with a fan base. Infused with distinct personalities, and a built-in cache of customers, Armstrong saw this as giving Monarch a unique advantage, if they could only capitalize on this market, which also catered to the wave of nostalgia marketing that was just taking off. That became Monarch's modus operandi as a company.

Monarch's first soft drink offering was Kickapoo Joy Juice, a citrus-flavored soda inspired by the tonic of the same name in Al Capp's *Li'l Abner*, the comic strip which appeared in newspapers from 1934 to 1977. Next, Monarch acquired Moxie. Armstrong, who had been an ad executive based in New York City, had made a number of trips to Massachusetts and Maine over the years, and was familiar with Moxie's loyal New England customer base. Both of these new acquisitions, steeped in nostalgia and with a ready made group of passionate customers, set the tone for Monarch's expanding portfolio.

Over the next two decades, Monarch continued to acquire new soft drink brands. Monarch did put some effort into regional marketing. The Moxie Horsemobile was restored, and began showing up at fairs, holiday parades, and other special events throughout New England. While this type of marketing made sense, tapping the nostalgic elements that Moxie played to, Monarch simultaneously made an odd decision, choosing to reformulate Moxie, concocting a caramel-colored version of the classic formula. The idea here was to find as many different ways to compete in an overly saturated cola market, against players with much, much deeper pockets for marketing.

By 1991, Monarch's portfolio included Kickapoo Joy Juice, Moxie, SunCrest, Mason's, Dr. Well's, Bubble Up, Dad's Old Fashioned Root Beer, and Quench.

Unfortunately, while Monarch grew and eventually came under the umbrella of ownership from a large French conglomerate, little was done to expand Moxie's niche. While Monarch now had more than 200 niche products, ranging across the carbonated, new age, and ready-to-drink categories, Moxie was becoming more difficult for fans to find, even in New England.

According to Frank Potter, in *The Book of Moxie*, "loyal Moxie drinkers in New England and Pennsylvania (where the drink had always been fairly easy to obtain) are experiencing considerable difficulty in finding Moxie in their favorite store—or any store for that matter."

While Frank Armstrong had close ties to Moxie, the company had been sold three or four times, and now Armstrong was long gone. As a result brands like Moxie no longer had direct marketing support and accountability. Worse, no one cared about their history and how to connect it to their fans, or how to reach a new generation of potential aficionados.

With the advent of the 21st century, Monarch became like many other companies that had been through the wave of mergers and acquisitions in the late 20th century. They had become nothing more than a company name on an investment prospectus. The company's strategy for Moxie was to maintain the trademark and collect brand royalties for any merchandise, but do little more.

Now owned by a large French conglomerate, Monarch had over 200 brands under its drink umbrella, and Moxie had gotten lost in the maze of drinks that company officials knew little about. While Moxie had its own festival, every summer, in Lisbon Falls, where tens of thousands of people descended on the town to celebrate the drink, turnover and inattention at Monarch made it nearly impossible for festival officials to find someone at Monarch to direct brand inquiries to, as well as address requests for marketing support.

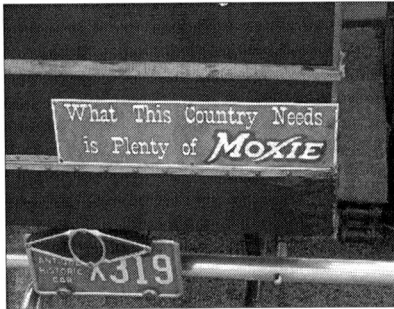

Moxie will solve our nation's ills

In early 2007, Moxie returned to its New England roots. Cornucopia Beverages Company, of Bedford, New Hampshire, bought the brand from Monarch and immediately began looking for ways to ramp up interest in Moxie.

The acquisition has been hailed by longtime fans of the unique drink. With the drink's fan base located primarily in New England and more specific, the northern reaches of the region, the Cornucopia acquisition seems like a good fit, at least initially, albeit, having the potential for some rockiness. Cornucopia happens to be a wholly-owned subsidiary of Coca-Cola of Northern New England (CCNNE). Moxie is also currently the only brand under the Cornucopia banner.

Cornucopia/CCNNE had worked with Monarch for years, prior to the acquisition, in a supplier/vendor arrangement. They had the exclusive territorial rights to distribute Moxie in New England. They also worked collaboratively on other brands, like All-Sport.

When Monarch began looking for companies that might be interested in brand spin offs, it allowed CCNNE to move from being a franchisee, to now having rights to the trademarked brand. This gave CCNNE real supply side advantages in acquiring Moxie.

On Patriot's Day, I drove to Bedford, to the Cornucopia/CCNNE corporate offices to speak with Justin Conroy, Cornucopia's brand manager. We spoke for about an hour about Moxie, Cornucopia's acquisition of the brand, and what the company's plans were for the future.

What follows are excerpts of that interview and insights into Moxie's possibilities for growth and expansion.

What were some of the considerations behind Cornucopia/CCNNE's acquisition of the Moxie Brand?

JC: *Monarch was a large French conglomerate, with a large stable of nostalgic brands; they had Dad's Root Beer, Bubble Up, Dr. Wells and of course Moxie. They also had All Sport, which was a newer brand. They were looking to divest everything. Because CCNNE sold the majority of Moxie—plus, we had worked collaboratively on* *some different drinks—we came up with the energy drink (All Sport) together, when they were looking to sell, they came to us; basically, with the first right of refusal, sort of.*

We held the franchise for a specific Moxie territory. When they (Monarch) were looking to sell, they offered us the right to purchase the brand. After working through all the details—it took a good nine months to hammer it out—by late March, it was like March 22, 2007, the deal closed. The technical owner of the brand is Cornucopia Beverages, which is a wholly-owned subsidary of CCNNE. This is mostly a contractual arrangement, but the only brand under the banner of Cornucopia is Moxie.

What is the attraction of Moxie to Cornucopia/CCNNE. Basically, why obtain this obscure regional brand?

JC: *Originally, it was when Monarch was going to spin it (Moxie) off; it was primarily a supply side play. It was integration—we were controlling the supply chain, giving us control of a trademark. It was basically letting us to get outside a box of just essentially being only a franchise operation. Because we had been such a large portion of doing the world's Moxie business, you never know what might happen if someone else controlled the brand. It was basically the best fit for it to come to us and for us to buy it. Monarch obvious recognized this.*

Is there a market for niche sodas?

JC: *There still is. You know, there's always a market. It's really not a niche, per se. We still sell a significant volume of it, inside the Northeast, alone. The hard part is for us to figure out a way to expand it. Just with our own efforts to put a little more focus and emphasis on Moxie, we made significant gains in volume, last year. There's definitely legs behind the brand, where it's recognized. The key is going to be to expand that recognition. The name just resonates. But there's a loss of people noticing, or remembering the drink; even out here and into Maine. A lot of people haven't tried it. There's no connection with the brand anymore, which is really a challenge for us, moving forward.*

What are some of the things that you've been able to do to expand availability?

JC: *The availability is actually very good in Maine. We've made some good gains; we've been able to secure authorization of 20 ounce Moxie in Cumberland Farms, this year. In Tedeschi (Store 24, Lil' Peach stores), where availability wasn't there before; these are two of the larger retailers in the region. We've always had it in Irving and in Big Apple before, for the more Maine-centric chains.*

How wide is the distribution of Moxie outside of New England?

JC: *There's a bottler in Catawissa, PA. They have a couple of counties out in there that they cover. There's a little bit of distribution in New York—kind of a continuation of our New England distribution—nothing in New York City. We've been able to secure a distribution through Sweet Bay Supermarkets, which is a 108 store chain, on the Gulf Coast side; these used be the old Kash n' Karry stores they are remodeling, down in Florida.*

There's some on the west coast. There's a bottler in Seattle and a co-packer outside of LA; their distribution isn't wide-ranging—they specialize in low-volume niche items, centered on nostalgia brands.

Does it matter where Moxie is bottled, as far as taste and quality is concerned?

JC: *The product (syrup) comes in five gallon jugs. There's a set formula that's included and you have to mete it to our specifications that are set, so that there's a consistent product. There should be no difference between a Moxie produced here in Londonderry (CCNNE's bottling location) and one produced by Polar in Worcester and one produced in Catawissa (PA). There shouldn't be any variation in taste or quality.*

How do you assure quality?

JC: *We have the ability to go in and audit at any time we want. That's part of the contract. If we were to go in and we found that it didn't meet specifications, then that's grounds for termination.*

Was last year (2007) your first year going to the Moxie Festival; what were some of your thoughts/observations?

JC: *It was my first year there. Other people had been there before. We kind of felt is was more important to go; we needed to be there to* *show our presence and commitment to fans of Moxie.*

It was kind of amazing to see so many people there. What's interesting about it is that it isn't all about the soda on that day, which is kind of unique, in its own sense. While it's about the brand, at the same time, it isn't. It's more just about the color orange and about the name, than anything else. It was a different take on the whole thing. I guess, having no idea about what it was going to be, it was just different—it's really hard to explain, really.

Talk a little bit about the NEMC and your relationship?

JC: *It got off to a kind of tenuous start…I don't know if tenuous is the right word. We really didn't know much about them, to be honest with you. It was a little bit weird, just because the Congress wanted to be intimately involved in our day-to-day operations. A lot of it was, we're just trying to get it (Moxie) off the ground and running and stuff, some of it, we just couldn't disclose—we're dealing with confidential contracting, you know? We can give you a little bit of what's going on, but not everything; I think they were a little hurt because we weren't as forthcoming as I think they thought we were going to be.*

The NEMC is amazingly protective of the brand; I'm not sure they understand the legalities of the trademark and the business side of the product. They feel it's their product.

JC: *I think they understand it and are aware of it, I just don't think they fully understand the intricate details when you start dealing with* *legal and trademark issues and everything that goes into acquiring a drink, like Moxie.*

Things with the Congress got off to a somewhat rocky start. We ruffled some feathers. Something happened on a trademark issue, something even bigger than that. We sent out a letter, based on some guy that was selling Moxie inside of a licensed area; first of all, it was a trademark infringement issue; second of all, it was a violation of a soft drink intrabrand, because it was into two franchise areas, protected by an act of Congress. We had to act on this information when it was brought to us. If we didn't, we're in jeopardy of losing the mark (the trademark) and losing any trademark value to it, because it's dilution, which is what they don't see from the outside.

It happened that the guy was 76-years-old, and was making it in his garage and so there are quality standards involved. Monarch had sold him a unit of concentrate in 2002, or 2003. Monarch was actually at fault, but never took care of it. He was going to use it, supposedly going to use it to make ice cream. But he was actually selling it, so that there is product liability indemnification involved, you know, so there were a wide list of reasons why we had to act upon it. That kind of irritated them; it irritated the Congress, because we were so aggressive. In retrospect, we probably were aggressive; we probably went about it the wrong way, with going at it by having our counsel send the letter, instead of having the letter coming from us, at Cornucopia, but we weren't sure how to do it. It was new to us and we knew we needed to protect the mark from a business sense. That definitely ruffled some feathers.

That's probably the toughest part. While we're trying to make decisions from a business perspective about the mark and they're looking at it as an advocacy group. I'm sure Merrill (Lewis, NEMC President) gets calls from people about the mark, because they don't know, thinking they're in charge of it. His card says 'president of the Moxie Congress.' We just need to have a clear line. The relationship has gotten better over time.

What are some of the marketing events that you are doing to publicize the Moxie brand?

JC: *We're doing a bunch of events. We're doing some 'guerilla' sampling events. We're trying to sample a wide variety of ages; a wide variety of genders; a wide variety of other demographics and try to seed it in as many places as we can.*

We've kind of taken the winter off, because in New England, it's harder to try to find large events that lend themselves well to these type of sampling events.

Last year, we did several ballpark events, like the Manchester Fisher Cats, Portland Sea Dogs. Also, Monhegan Sun. We'll be doing some store events, Loudon International Speedway. We try to get events set up where we can get a good amount of traffic flow coming through.

I always thought Moxie broke out along demographic lines. Do you feel an urgency to reach a younger demographic with Moxie?

JC: *Not really. It's one of those things, like Tab. Tab's remained steady across demographic lines. There's no explanation as to why Tab should have remained steady across different age groups. I think people remember a brand. Packaging comes into the equation. Nowadays, people are looking for things that are different and I think that's our largest point of differentiation—it's different; it's unique—that's what we have going for us.*

At the same time, all those things are great, but you have nothing to compare it to. What's it taste like? It's a root beer; it's a cola?People are not quite sure how to define it.

[Authors note: I had always thought that Moxie broke out along demographic lines. Conroy, however, doesn't think that. Currently, the company is sampling a wide demographic, attempting to "seed" the drink within New England.-JB]

Do you see Moxie ever breaking out of its regional ghetto?

JB: *I guess long-term, we'd like to see Moxie succeed. I know that's kind of vague, but you try to achieve what's best for the brand. Is that a super-regional product, or are we going to be able to achieve eastern seaboard penetration? You try to match profiles and tastes.*

There's a southern drink, Cheer Wine that's similar to Moxie. It's a cherry cola flavor that's immensely popular in the south. Still, it's never really been able to break out of that southern region, but you don't know if that's their goal, if that's part of their growth plan, or if it's a flavor profile, or if that's just where they want to stay. But they have the merchandise; they have the nostalgia, so they have everything that seems to fit their business profile.

We're looking at demographic information, but a lot of what we're doing is 'gut.' We can analyze scientific and demographic material and data, but at the end of the day, we are asking, what is it we want to do?

We're focused on being strong where we're strongest; there's still a lot of room for growth in New England, so that bodes well, rather than just dumping it in a market where we might not do as well.

Can you tap the nostalgia of Moxie, or does that work against you?

JC: *I'm not sure. Does nostalgia work in going to new media; how does nostalgia transcend ongoing viral? As you start trying to go 360, on a media strategy, does nostalgia really work? These are things we need to think about. Our goal is to try to tap into this subculture that Moxie plays well to.*

There is a concern among members of the NEMC that we're trying to make Moxie ubiquitous. We aren't, but at the same time, we are trying to find new groups of people; we're trying to reach out to this subculture that identifies with Moxie. I mean, if we aren't able to grow and sustain it that means that it could eventually die.

Any plans for large national marketing campaigns, such as hosting a bowl game, like Dr. Pepper?

JC: *Way too cost prohibitive. We get calls from local race car drivers; the amount they're asking for to just do three or four races is astronomical.*

Marketing today is done on such a large scale. To buy even traditional media (print, radio, television), you have to invest substantial amounts. We've been offered opportunities, but can we justify it. What is our ROI in doing this?

We are really in a start up phase. Moxie, for us, is like a brand new product. Monarch did nothing. Even their camera-ready artwork is so dated, we can't use it. It's unbelievable.

We don't even have stuff for cooler doors; promotional stuff.

Just an example of what we're up against; The UPC had to be changed; original UPC was tied to Monarch. That was a large task and an expensive one. You end up having to send it to a design house; we upgraded our own packaging in the process. The new 8 ounce package is new; we thought that Moxie might play to the older demographic, but also, the health care segment is an area that we are targeting.

Marketing is a challenge, but I'm optimistic that we're on the right track, with Moxie.

Justin, thank you for your time.

JC: *It was my pleasure.*

Chapter 6

The Congress of Moxie

Moxie has its own history, books about its beginnings, and even a law, recognizing it as Maine's official soft drink. With all that, Moxie certainly has to have a band of zealots and fans—the drink's official fan club. Enter the New England Moxie Congress (NEMC).

The NEMC, or The Congress, for short, officially held their first meeting in July, 1991. They began as a small group of Moxie drinkers (and some that weren't) that were interested in the phenomenon that was Moxie.

According to Congress historian, John Lehaney, "We're a fairly diverse group." Lehaney, a retired community college counselor, who lives in Missouri, travels back to New England every summer, in July, to attend the variety of Moxie events that happen each year.

Like many of the Congress, Lehaney's passionate about Moxie and has taken it upon himself to compile a four volume history of the Congress, housed at the Matthews Museum of Maine Heritage, in Union, Maine, which is where visitors will find a sizable collection of Moxie memorabilia and other assorted Moxie-related items, including the Moxie Bottle House.

"I began working on the history and it continues to grow," said Lehaney. "I'm now up to four volumes, and over four-hundred pages."

Lehaney's own appreciation for Moxie and its unique characteristics began in New England. He was born and grew up in Leominster, Massachusetts and remembers the days when the soda clerk would mix up your soda, right in front of your eyes.

As to the beginnings of the NEMC, Lehaney says the origins were small.

"We began with twenty-two charter members. Not all of the first attendees (at the first meeting in 1991) liked Moxie. In the beginning, we were a very weak organization, but over time, we've gotten stronger."

He's quick to credit a number of people for this.

"Kurt Kabelic, a retired Cornell University professor, has been a driving force behind strengthening our organization. He helped organize our membership, and develop our member's list."

According to Lehaney, the Congress has 229 people on its membership list. Not all of these members are as energized as the others, however.

"I'd say we have about twenty-two, to twenty-four members that are really involved. Merrill Lewis has become a great leader of our organization. George and Judy Gross, who live in New Jersey and also have a home in Maine, they might be our hardest workers, particularly trying to raise the necessary funding to restore the Bottle House."

Lehaney is encouraged by Cornucopia's recent acquisition of Moxie, bringing the brand back to New England.

"We all want them to succeed. I'm not sure if we can expect much more than it (Moxie) being successful in New England, at this point."

Come July, once again, Lehaney, and his wife Barbara, will fly into Hartford; they'll rent a vehicle to drive up to Maine, and make their Moxie pilgrimage. They visit in July because this is when most of the various Moxie happenings occur in the area.

"I have my own Missouri Moxie vanity plate that I attach to the rental car. My wife thinks I'm going to get into trouble, but I've never had a problem, yet. We come to the festival, in Lisbon Falls on Saturday and then, head down to the Trolley Museum, in Kennebunkport, for our annual meeting for Moxie."

Lehaney credits his involvement with the NEMC for some great friendships and a fun way to celebrate a really special drink.

"We look forward to our trip in July every year and Moxie makes that possible."

Congress member's Moxie collection

Merrill Lewis is the president of the NEMC, assuming that role in 2005, taking over from Don Worthen. Lewis' first experience with Moxie, like many, was when he was a youngster.

"I drank Moxie as a kid—I liked it—I thought it had a different taste; a little more bite than other sodas, but it was just a soda to me."

After graduating from the University of New Hampshire, in 1967, he moved to Syracuse, New York, taking a position with Carrier, where he worked as an engineer. There was no Moxie to be found. When he'd return home to Manchester for a visit, he'd pick up a supply and bring some back. Lewis became a Moxie missionary, trying to interest others in the drink. During that time, he started collecting some of the various cans, as Moxie had changed the design. Family members became aware of his interest.

Asked about how he went from casual consumer, to increasingly more invested in Moxie and its history, eventually becoming an aficionado of the culture that surrounds the drink, Lewis mentioned a series of events.

"I had moved back here (to New England) and two or three things happened. I got Frank Potter's book for Christmas. My daughter-in-law picked it up at a flea market. I looked at it and thought, 'This is quite a book,' with all the collectibles and memorabilia, so that kind of whetted my appetite."

A friend of Lewis' happened to be traveling in Maine, and saw a sign advertising a meeting of a Moxie club. He later mentioned it to him. The meeting was being held at the Seashore Trolley Museum, in Kennebunkport. Lewis decided to make the trek and attend the meeting.

"I went to the meeting and at that time, I knew nothing about the goings-on in Lisbon Falls. I showed up and all these people are dressed in orange t-shirts. I asked them where they got them and they told me, 'Lisbon Falls.' I asked them, 'What's going on in Lisbon Falls?'"

Lewis found out that this group was enthusiastic about Moxie and that they regularly attended the festival in Lisbon Falls, and other events and he just got caught up in it. Lewis would attend his very first Moxie Festival in July of 1999.

Coincidentally that same year, Lewis purchased a place in his hometown of Manchester, New Hampshire, on Pine Island Pond. Across the pond had been a well-known amusement park, where the original Moxie Bottle House was located and happened to still be intact.

"I actually bought this house (his current domicile) that next year and it was the first I heard about the Moxie Bottle House and it happened to be just down the road. Not only did I have a nice waterfront property in the middle of the city, but the Moxie Bottle House is just down the road. Aren't I a hot shit." Lewis can't help but laugh at the coincidence, before adding, "Then, the next year, they started tearing it down."

Lewis noticed that the shingles were coming off; the original Moxie label was exposed. He went down to investigate and found out that the Congress was involved in taking it apart and moving it. Because he was so close, members of the NEMC asked if he'd be willing to write a history of the house, and the project.

"I told them I was an engineer, not a historian. I also realize I'm compulsive and addictive, so I got into the project, all four feet and the trough and did research on The Bottle House. I learned the history of Moxie, how The Bottle House went with it, the history of the NEMC and I was hooked."

Lewis recognizes the importance of Frank Anicetti and the connection that Moxie now has with Lisbon Falls and its annual Moxie Festival. He also understands that the festival represents a regional festival, connected with groups like the Chamber of Commerce. It attracts people, helps the town, and he sees Frank's store as the center of all of it."

"I've been thinking lately about Frank's store and his role in the festival and what happens to the festival, if Frank and his store go off the face of the map. Chances are, the festival would probably continue for a few years, but its his store and Frank himself that have become the focal point. He's the one that people want to see. Frank's the one that's been written up and all that. The Moxie Congress, per se, which came after the festival started, as a formal group, participates and for years—and still do—have had a special position in the parade. We bring our horsemobiles. I have my replica of The Moxie Bottle House. We bring our collectibles and other memorabilia and then we depart for our clambake, down to Freeport."

We've tried to find a way to have our own event and stay in Lisbon, or Lisbon Falls, but the logistics just don't work out. Every alternative that I've tried to come up with in talking with Sue (Conroy) and others always ends up conflicting with other things, like the Friday night fireman's event and now, the fireworks. Plus, we really like our spot in Freeport (Winslow Park)."

Lewis downplays any supposed friction between the NEMC and the festival committee in Lisbon Falls. They're choice of Freeport, for their clambake, and the Trolley Museum, for the annual meeting, are much more to do with practicality and logistics, than any aversion or design that members of the Congress have to move the festival out of Lisbon Falls.

"I've heard mumblings about 'Why does the NEMC always have to have their stuff somewhere else?' It's all about logistics, that's all. Personally, I think the Trolley Museum hurts us some, with our meeting. We've looked at a variety of options and we just haven't been able to make Lisbon Falls work for us. The festival is run by the Chamber of Commerce, and what they decide they want to do, is what happens. I've talked to Sue about different issues, like last year's t-shirt episode (where a few vendors were undercutting Anicetti's t-shirt prices). We understand and respect what Frank's done and does and we've agreed that no one other than Frank and possibly Sue, will be selling any t-shirts, or hats, with a Moxie logo."

As president, Lewis continues to find new ways to grow interest in Moxie and in particular, the NEMC. Being involved in Lisbon Falls is part of that strategy, as Lewis understands that you need to have your events in places where people will go to. The annual crowds are evidence that the town is the right location for the annual festival.

Wrapping up our interview, I asked Lewis about what his thoughts are about Moxie's future. Is it just a nostalgic nod to the past, or will a new generation of Moxie drinkers get hooked, just like he had?

"I think Moxie's base is there. Our objective is to make people aware of it and we're interested in Moxie's continuance without changes in its basic formula. We're not opposed to new packaging, or new products being developed. What we want to make sure of, however, is that we can still get the traditional drink. That's our objective—the continuity of it."

Lewis hopes that Cornucopia will take a more active role in publicizing the drink. He sees potential for Moxie's growth outside of the regional niche. In order to do this, he feels that Cornucopia/CCNNE needs to be more aggressive in their marketing and outreach.

Jim Jansson found his way to Moxie through a fourth grade classmate and an introduction to *Mad Magazine*. The magazine, known for its groundbreaking parodies, and sentimental fondness for the familiar staples of American culture, would seem an appropriate vehicle for young Jansson to find the Moxie logo, inserted sans logic, into a variety of drawings.

In *The Stories Behind The Moxie Collage*, Jansson's own self-published take on his Moxie stories and other Moxie lore writes, "I first saw the Moxie logo in the magazine in 1958." From his own research, Jansson was able to determine that the Moxie logo first appeared in *Mad*, in issue #43, which was released in December, 1958. As to the rationale behind this odd appearance of the Moxie logo, Jansson extrapolates that this may have been *Mad's* experiment with subliminal advertising.

He writes, "Obviously, the subliminal use of the Moxie logo in Mad worked. Forty-five years later, I'm still drinking Moxie and I'm a member of the New England Moxie Congress because of it!"

Jansson first found out about the Moxie Festival, in Lisbon Falls, from Joe Veillieux's website, in 2002. The year before, he had also read Frank Potter's, *The Moxie Mystique*.

"The Potter book was written in 1981, so I figured that probably all the Moxie stuff had died out, over the past 20 years," said Jansson, over the phone. "I was intrigued when I saw the festival mentioned on the website, so I told my wife that we should visit Maine, in July."

Not expecting much, both he and his wife were surprised by what they found when they rolled into Lisbon Falls on parade day, 2002.

"We were pleasantly surprised and actually amazed by what we saw. Being from Connecticut, we thought this would be a local festival, with a few hundred people at best."

Instead, the Janssons were greeted by a crowd of probably more than twenty thousand people, a huge parade, with floats, marching bands, clowns, and a variety of other elements in Maine's largest parade.

"Both my wife and I were hooked by that first visit and have been coming ever since. 2008 will be our seventh consecutive year."

That first festival, in 2002, was where Jansson came up with the idea of assembling photo collages of the photos he took of the various elements of the festival. When he returned in 2003, he brought with him his very first edition of 10 signed and numbered collages.

While Jansson has discontinued this after doing it for four successive years ("They were just too much work"), these collages captured some of the key movers and shakers of the Moxie world, like Frank Potter, Frank Anicetti, Wil Markey (Moxie

Horsemobile), Don Worthen (former NEMC president), and others.

"Being able to meet and get to know these people has lent extra meaning to putting these together."

In addition to creating the collages, Jansson added an additional dimension to his involvement with the Moxie Festival—he decided to show up, dressed as the Moxie Boy, which Jansson believes, is the only live representation of this iconic Moxie figure, since his inception, in 1907.

"I have to give Joe Veillieux a lot of the credit for the success of [the Moxie collage]. He had put pictures on his website a couple of weeks before the Moxie Festival. I had sent these to Joe and told him he was free to use them in his book he was planning to publish. Unbeknownst to me, he had them up on the web and I got some great advance PR!"

Jansson has enjoyed his involvement with the NEMC and has found a group of people equally passionate abut Moxie, who enjoy being part of the festival, each year in Lisbon Falls. He credits the group for trying to promote Moxie, first and foremost.

"There is something about the festival and Moxie that captures a sense of time past. It's like a lost piece of Americana that people are searching for. We've met people from all over the country that also come each year, to Lisbon Falls, for the Moxie Festival. We really feel like Lisbon Falls has become a second home for us, just from coming to the festival."

For regular attendees of the annual Moxie Festival, in Lisbon Falls, they've grown familiar with a sad-faced clown, named

Taurus. Patterned after some of the classic clown faces of the past, Taurus goes back to the beginning of the Moxie Festival and beyond, all the way back to the Frontier Days parades of the 60s and 70s.

Fred Goldrup, the same person who came up with the idea of passing a bill to make Moxie the official soft drink of Maine, is a Moxie Festival regular, and has been making people laugh for fifty years, with his alter ego, Taurus. Goldrup has a congenital ear condition that has left him deaf in one ear, and possessing only fifteen percent hearing in his other. This hasn't stopped the born performer from regaling young and old alike with his various routines, each and every year, in Lisbon Falls, however.

Goldrup doesn't recall his first taste of Moxie, but like many of his generation, Moxie was always around. He mentioned several sodas and popular drinks that were around before Coke and Pepsi consolidated the soft drink market.

"I always just had Moxie. But, over the years, I've noticed the change in taste. Remember Orange Crush? Real crushed orange pulp. Pineapple soda, too. There was a grapefruit soda that I recall—Squirt. That had a 'real' taste. Squirt! The original Moxie taste has changed. It's more metallic. I think that big change came when the government said sassafras was not good, and removed as an ingredient. When the government lifted the ban, the Moxie formula remained as it currently is. The diet Moxie is closer to the bitter-sweet taste I remember. I think it's too sweet today."

Goldrup still has fond memories of being the primary person responsible for the Moxie bill.

"I was allowed to testify when the State had hearings. I was pleased Senator Lois Snowe-Mello joined us to testify in favor of the bill. She is known as 'Betty Boop' to friends. She is quite a lady! By the way, did Senator Rotundo tell you she DOES NOT like Moxie? I could not believe that. A number of Letters to the Editor panned the State for wasting time on such a bill when there were more important things to do. I enjoyed testifying. Against ALL rules, I had a can of Moxie in my pocket when I spoke, removing the can from my pocket, snapping the ring, I said, 'To your good health,' and toasted the Committee! Signs forbade food or beverages in the Committee room. It was taken in good humor and I wasn't arrested."

Goldrup credits Emmett Kelly (famous tramp clown of Ringling Bros. and Barnum & Bailey Circus fame; later a Brooklyn Dodgers mascot) as a hero and inspiration, in the development of Taurus, over fifty years ago. He reminisced about his very first appearance, as Taurus, at the Wales Grange, back in 1953.

"I liked the way Taurus made sad things funny. He was mostly pantomime. It was a challenge to do magic in pantomime because a magician needs to misdirect the audience's attention in order to do a bit of sleight-of-hand. I learned early on that I had an impossible mission. My first appearance was 20 minutes long. I teased a couple of girls in the audience by shining a flashlight through an empty tube to show it was empty. The girls loved this guy! I had fun—I focused on them while performing to everyone at the hall. Behind the painted face and long straggly hair, no one knew this was a 19-year-old egotist making his first appearance."

Taurus the Clown has performed all over the state of Maine, including the critically-acclaimed Maine Festival, during its heyday, at Bowdoin College. At seventy-four, and after five decades of performing, Taurus could be excused if he decided to hang up his costume. He might very well be on the sidelines, if not for Anicetti and his annual request that Goldrup join the parade. With age and its accompanying infirmities, Goldrup looks to adapt his routine and still participate in any way he can.

"You know, if it weren't for Frank, Taurus would have been out in moth balls. He hears things no one would tell me. Frank tells me that people would miss seeing me if I didn't show up. He tells me people love to see me holding court with people in the back of the store. I hope this year he will have a chair with a back for me. With two vertebrae out of alignment and two deteriorating discs, I need to lean back. Last year all he had was a stool, and the pain in my back was torture! I will see if I can find a folding chair and hide it in the back room a day or two before the Parade."

I found the various stories of my subjects fascinating—like Merrill Lewis' journey—which in many ways, mirrored my own introduction to Moxie, with the portal being a childhood memory of the drink. From there, Potter's book helped Lewis (and me), gain an understanding of the depth of the history, and the culture that surrounds Moxie. There are many compelling hooks that capture people, just like Lewis and I, and as a result, they become fans of Moxie for a lifetime. Groups like the NEMC help facilitate that deeper relationship with Moxie that's much more than just an affinity for a soft drink.

For countless people that come to Lisbon Falls, for the festival, Moxie is about orange and ice cream and other attendant festival activities. Almost everyone is aware, to some degree about Moxie's connection, but they're not quite sure what it is and why Lisbon Falls is the axis of connection. For many, they believe that Moxie was invented in Lisbon Falls. Others probably think that Frank Anicetti bottles Moxie in the basement of the The House of Moxie. For a few, they pick up Potter's book, or might buy this one and like Merrill Lewis, John Lehaney, Fred Goldrup, Jim Jansson, and others, they become hooked, taking a deeper look at Moxie and the culture that surrounds it.

Potter and Will Markey swapping Moxie stories

Chapter 7

Moxie Essential Reading

The Moxie Mystique, by Frank N. Potter (1981)

This is the book that began the modern era of Moxie, the vintage drink that started as a nerve tonic, in 1876. Potter's book is the book to christen your quest in understanding the cult of Moxie and beginning your own journey to deeper Moxie knowledge.

Combining elements of memorabilia, legend, and historical authentication in a very readable book of 144 pages, Potter gives you a thorough primer to take you from Moxie neophyte to becoming known as the Moxie guy in your social network. If you know nothing about Moxie, *The Moxie Mystique* is the important first step in getting your Moxie shwerve on.

Recognizing Moxie's natural nostalgic tie-in, Potter does an excellent job combining the nostalgia, with the history of Moxie's beginnings as a nerve food. Potter also takes the time to supply details on Moxie's founder, Dr. Augustin Thompson, from Union, Maine, as well as Frank Archer, America's pioneering marketer and entrepreneur, who rarely missed an opportunity to market Moxie to America's masses.

It was Potter's book signing in Lisbon Falls, on June 13, 1982 that launched what we know as The Moxie Festival. Five-hundred people jammed Frank Anicetti's store, now known as The House of Moxie, primarily as a result of that event.

Potter became the quintessential Moxie spokesman on the basis of his book, regularly speaking around the country, as well as making his way back to Lisbon Falls frequently, to be parade grand marshall, or hawk books. At ninety-five, Potter's travel is limited, so Moxie fans will have to settle for his books for a sense of the man.

Potter's a good writer and transcends the pitfalls of lesser lights that lack the ability to tackle subjects like Moxie, without getting bogged down in detail and minutia. To his credit, he is true to the history, but his prose flows effortlessly, making *The Moxie Mystique* such a valuable book, capturing the vast landscape that is Moxie.

The Moxie Encyclopedia, Volume I; Q. David Bowers, (1985)

The Moxie Encyclopedia, Volume I, by Q. David Bowers, has been an indispensable research tool for me. Bowers deliver over seven-hundred pages of thoroughly researched and well-documented pages on every facet of the Moxie phenomenon. On top of all of that, Bowers even includes an index.

From a research perspective, Bowers' material is more valuable, versus the material from Frank Potter. It's obvious that Bowers spent the extra time to pull the various facets of Moxie together in a way that no one has since and probably won't be bothered to do in the future.

The Moxie Encyclopedia, Volume I, intimates that there is, or might be, a Volume II. I'm intrigued by this. As a researcher,

I can't imagine the hours that Bowers has invested in this first volume. I also find it hard to believe that as thorough as it is that there are still stones unturned and that this additional material is going to reveal new information on Moxie.

My hat's off to Mr. Bowers, for his valuable service to all things Moxie.

The Book of Moxie, Frank N. Potter (1987)

This is Frank Potter's follow-up to his first book, *The Moxie Mystique*, which was the one that helped put him on the map as Moxie expert. This book is the perfect introduction to someone who knows little, or nothing about Moxie. As a research tool, it pales in comparison when placed alongside Bowers' work, particularly for anyone doing extensive research on Moxie's history. Potter writes history for the common man, which in its own right is a gift and a valuable service. Speaking of gifts, *The Book of Moxie* makes a perfect book to give friends and family, particularly those who always ask, "Why do you care about Moxie, so much?"

The Book of Moxie's great contribution is that it builds upon *The Moxie Mystique* and provides greater detail and a wider historical arc than the first one, which is important for a drink that goes back to 1884.

Both Bowers' book and Potter's books have their unique qualities. The average person would probably be intimidated by Bower's thorough to a fault treatment of Moxie. Potter's style, which caters more to entertainment, with a measure of Moxie education thrown in, would probably be a better first introduction.

The Book of Moxie is perfect for the coffee table, with a large number of vintage photos that makes it perfect for thumbing through and reading at one's leisure.

Potter's book is, as he describes it, is "an overall picture" an almost day-to-day stream of activity, struggles, gains, setbacks, clashes of purpose; but most of all, the heart that went into the most fascinating soda pop endeavor in American history."

Moxie, since 1884, by Joseph Veillieux

Veillieux's book, which came out in 2003, is my least favorite of the books detailing Moxie's history. It's worth owning for Moxie completists, collectors, and those seeking Moxie memorabilia, but the information is all available in much better formats.

While Bowers' book, and Potter's two books are laid out professionally and extra care was taken to secure quality printing and presentation, the Veillieux book is less well put together than the previous works on Moxie.

The most valuable aspect of the book is the last sections on collectibles, and Veillieux's biggest contribution is his pricing of the various items. The original $30 price tag of the book, however, makes it a pricey collector's catalog, in my opinion. I would suggest looking for it at a discounted price, as it isn't worth the hefty list price.

Author and Anicetti discussing Moxie

below left: Roy Skillings and Al Smith compare beards

below right: Youngster Dustin Watson loves Moxie, 1989

Jim Baumer is a Moxie drinker and grew up in Lisbon Falls. He cares deeply about small communities and the people who inhabit them. This is his second book and follow-up to the award-winning, *When Towns Had Teams*, which celebrated the heyday of town team baseball in Maine. He resides across the river from Lisbon Falls, in Durham, with his lovely wife, Mary and their Sheltie, Bernie, who is old and deaf, and who will eat anything, but does not like carbonated drinks—Moxie included.

Author and Frank Anicetti giving the Moxie Finger